Scott Foresman
SCIENCE

Series Authors

Dr. Timothy Cooney
Professor of Earth Science and
*   Science Education*
Earth Science Department
University of Northern Iowa
Cedar Falls, Iowa

Michael Anthony DiSpezio
Science Education Specialist
Cape Cod Children's Museum
Falmouth, Massachusetts

Barbara K. Foots
Science Education Consultant
Houston, Texas

Dr. Angie L. Matamoros
Science Curriculum Specialist
Broward County Schools
Ft. Lauderdale, Florida

Kate Boehm Nyquist
Science Writer and Curriculum Specialist
Mount Pleasant, South Carolina

Dr. Karen L. Ostlund
Professor
Science Education Center
The University of Texas at Austin
Austin, Texas

Contributing Authors

Dr. Anna Uhl Chamot
Associate Professor and
*   ESL Faculty Advisor*
Department of Teacher Preparation
    and Special Education
Graduate School of Education
    and Human Development
The George Washington University
Washington, DC

Dr. Jim Cummins
Professor
Modern Language Centre and
    Curriculum Department
Ontario Institute for Studies in Education
Toronto, Canada

Gale Philips Kahn
Lecturer, Science and Math Education
Elementary Education Department
California State University, Fullerton
Fullerton, California

Vincent Sipkovich
Teacher
Irvine Unified School District
Irvine, California

Steve Weinberg
Science Consultant
Connecticut State
    Department of Education
Hartford, Connecticut

Scott Foresman

Editorial Offices: Glenview, Illinois · Parsippany, New Jersey · New York, New York
Sales Offices: Parsippany, New Jersey · Duluth, Georgia · Glenview, Illinois
Carrollton, Texas · Ontario, California
www.sfscience.com

Content Consultants

Dr. J. Scott Cairns
National Institutes of Health
Bethesda, Maryland

Jackie Cleveland
Elementary Resource Specialist
Mesa Public School District
Mesa, Arizona

Robert L. Kolenda
Science Lead Teacher, K-12
Neshaminy School District
Langhorne, Pennsylvania

David P. Lopath
Teacher
The Consolidated School District
   of New Britain
New Britain, Connecticut

Sammantha Lane Magsino
Science Coordinator
Institute of Geophysics
University of Texas at Austin
Austin, Texas

Kathleen Middleton
Director, Health Education
ToucanEd
Soquel, California

Irwin Slesnick
Professor of Biology
Western Washington University
Bellingham, Washington

Dr. James C. Walters
Professor of Geology
University of Northern Iowa
Cedar Falls, Iowa

Multicultural Consultants

Dr. Shirley Gholston Key
Assistant Professor
University of Houston-Downtown
Houston, Texas

Damon L. Mitchell
Quality Auditor
Louisiana-Pacific Corporation
Conroe, Texas

Classroom Reviewers

Kathleen Avery
Teacher
Kellogg Science/Technology
   Magnet
Wichita, Kansas

Margaret S. Brown
Teacher
Cedar Grove Primary
Williamston, South Carolina

Deborah Browne
Teacher
Whitesville Elementary School
Moncks Corner, South Carolina

Wendy Capron
Teacher
Corlears School
New York, New York

Jiwon Choi
Teacher
Corlears School
New York, New York

John Cirrincione
Teacher
West Seneca Central Schools
West Seneca, New York

Jacqueline Colander
Teacher
Norfolk Public Schools
Norfolk, Virginia

Dr. Terry Contant
Teacher
Conroe Independent
   School District
The Woodlands, Texas

Susan Crowley-Walsh
Teacher
Meadowbrook Elementary School
Gladstone, Missouri

Charlene K. Dindo
Teacher
Fairhope K-1 Center/Pelican's
   Nest Science Lab
Fairhope, Alabama

Laurie Duffee
Teacher
Barnard Elementary
Tulsa, Oklahoma

Beth Anne Ebler
Teacher
Newark Public Schools
Newark, New Jersey

Karen P. Farrell
Teacher
Rondout Elementary School District
   #72
Lake Forest, Illinois

Anna M. Gaiter
Teacher
Los Angeles Unified School District
   Los Angeles Systemic Initiative
Los Angeles, California

Federica M. Gallegos
Teacher
Highland Park Elementary
   Salt Lake School District
Salt Lake City, Utah

Janet E. Gray
Teacher
Anderson Elementary - Conroe ISD
Conroe, Texas

Karen Guinn
Teacher
Ehrhardt Elementary School - KISD
Spring, Texas

Denis John Hagerty
Teacher
Al Ittihad Private Schools
Dubai, United Arab Emirates

Judith Halpern
Teacher
Bannockburn School
Deerfield, Illinois

Debra D. Harper
Teacher
Community School District 9
Bronx, New York

Gretchen Harr
Teacher
Denver Public Schools - Doull School
Denver, Colorado

Bonnie L. Hawthorne
Teacher
Jim Darcy School
   School Dist #1
Helena, Montana

Marselle Heywood-Julian
Teacher
Community School District 6
New York, New York

Scott Klene
Teacher
Bannockburn School 106
Bannockburn, Illinois

Thomas Kranz
Teacher
Livonia Primary School
Livonia, New York

Tom Leahy
Teacher
Coos Bay School District
Coos Bay, Oregon

Mary Littig
Teacher
Kellogg Science/Technology
   Magnet
Wichita, Kansas

Patricia Marin
Teacher
Corlears School
New York, New York

Susan Maki
Teacher
Cotton Creek CUSD 118
Island Lake, Illinois

Efraín Meléndez
Teacher
East LA Mathematics Science
   Center LAUSD
Los Angeles, California

Becky Mojalid
Teacher
Manarat Jeddah Girls' School
Jeddah, Saudi Arabia

Susan Nations
Teacher
Sulphur Springs Elementary
Tampa, Florida

Brooke Palmer
Teacher
Whitesville Elementary
Moncks Corner, South Carolina

Jayne Pedersen
Teacher
Laura B. Sprague
   School District 103
Lincolnshire, Illinois

Shirley Pfingston
Teacher
Orland School Dist 135
Orland Park, Illinois

Teresa Gayle Rountree
Teacher
Box Elder School District
Brigham City, Utah

Helen C. Smith
Teacher
Schultz Elementary
Klein Independent School District
Tomball, Texas

Denette Smith-Gibson
Teacher
Mitchell Intermediate, CISD
The Woodlands, Texas

Mary Jean Syrek
Teacher
Dr. Charles R. Drew Science
   Magnet
Buffalo, New York

Rosemary Troxel
Teacher
Libertyville School District 70
Libertyville, Illinois

Susan D. Vani
Teacher
Laura B. Sprague School
School District 103
Lincolnshire, Illinois

Debra Worman
Teacher
Bryant Elementary
Tulsa, Oklahoma

Dr. Gayla Wright
Teacher
Edmond Public School
Edmond, Oklahoma

ISBN: 0-328-03422-3

Copyright © 2003, Pearson Education, Inc.

4 5 6 7 8 9 10 V057 06 05 04 03

Unit A
Life Science

Unit B
Physical Science

Unit C
Earth Science

Unit D
Human Body

Your Science Handbook

Using Scientific Methods for Science Inquiry

Scientists use scientific methods to find answers to questions. Scientific methods have the steps shown on these pages. Scientists sometimes use the steps in different order. You can use these steps for your own science inquiries.

Problem
The problem is the question you want to answer. Inquiry has led to many discoveries in science. Ask your question.

How does the amount of water in a bottle affect the sound made when the bottle is tapped?

Give your hypothesis.
Tell what you think the answer is to the problem.

If the amount of water is more, then the sound will be lower when the bottle is tapped. ▶

Control the variables.
Change one thing when you test your hypothesis. Keep everything else the same.

Test your hypothesis.

Do experiments to test your hypothesis. You may need to do experiments more than one time to see if the results are the same each time.

> I'll tap each bottle with a pencil and observe the sound.

Collect your data.

Collect data about the problem. Record your data on a chart. You might make drawings or write words or sentences.

Tell your conclusion.

Compare your results and hypothesis. Decide if your hypothesis is right or wrong. Tell what you decide.

> The more water in the bottle, the lower the pitch of the sound.

? Inquire Further

Use what you learn to answer other problems or questions. You may want to do your experiment again or change your experiment.

▲ Does the size of a bottle affect the sound made when the bottle is tapped?

Using Process Skills for Science Inquiry

Scientists use process skills to do research. You will use process skills when you do the activities in this book.

When you test something, you use process skills. When you collect data, you use process skills. When you make conclusions and tell what you learn, you use process skills.

Observing

Your senses are seeing, hearing, smelling, touching, and tasting. Use your senses to find out about objects or things that happen.

Communicating

Use words, pictures, charts, and graphs to share what you learn.

Classifying

Sort or group objects by their properties.

Estimating and Measuring

Estimate means to tell what you think about an object's measurement is. Make an estimate. Then measure the object.

Inferring

Make a conclusion or a guess from what you observe or from what you already know.

I think it is a...

Predicting

Tell what you think will happen.

Making Definitions

Use what you already know to describe something or tell what it means.

Making and Using Models

Make a model to show what you know about something.

Giving Hypotheses

Make a statement you can test to answer a problem or a question.

Collecting Data

Record what you observe and measure. Use graphs, charts, pictures, or words. Use what you learned to answer problems or questions.

Controlling Variables

Change one thing that may affect what happens. Keep everything else the same.

Experimenting

Plan and do an investigation to test a hypothesis or to answer a problem. Then make conclusions.

 Science Inquiry

As you use your science book, you will ask questions, do investigations, answer your questions, and then tell others what you learned. This is called science inquiry. You can use science inquiry to do this science project.

> What can affect how long it takes a wet paper towel to dry?

1 **Ask a question about living things, objects, or things that happen.**

What can affect how long it takes a wet paper towel to dry?

2 **Plan and do a simple investigation to answer your question.**

Put a few drops of water on each of several paper towels. Test different ways to make the paper towels dry.

3 **Use some simple materials and tools to help you.**

Use a dropper to put water on each paper towel. Use a clock to time how long it takes each paper towel to dry. Make a chart to show the steps in your experiment.

4 **Use what you observed to answer your question.**

What affected how long it took for your paper towels to dry?

5 **Share your information with your class.**

You can use words or pictures.

Unit A
Life Science

Science and Technology
In Your World!

Can an airplane plant a tree?

Yes! Each plastic cone in the picture is filled with soil and a small tree. The cone is dropped from a plane and sticks in the ground. Then the tree grows.

Chapter 1
Plants

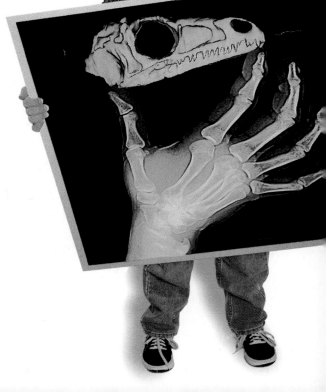

What kind of animal has a long neck made of metal?

It's a giraffe in the Robot Zoo! The animals in the Robot Zoo look and move like real animals. Yet they are all made of metal machine parts.

Chapter 2
Animals

What can scientists learn from dinosaur bones?

Scientists use X-rays and other machines to learn about dinosaur bones. The bones can tell scientists how big the animal's eyes were, and how well it was able to hear and smell.

Chapter 3
Fossils

Chapter 1
Plants

How Did That Plant Get There?

🎵 Sing to the tune of *Where, Oh Where Has My Little Dog Gone?*

How, oh how did that plant get there?

It must have started from seed.

There's a stem, some leaves, and a bud on top,

And it's growing at a fast speed.

How, oh how did that plant get there?

And now what else does it need?

It needs air and water and light to grow,

On that we all can agree.

But, how, oh how did that plant get there?

It makes me wonder indeed.

Was it wind or water or maybe a bird

That dropped off a traveling seed?

Original lyrics by Gerri Brioso and Richard Freitas.
Produced by Children's Television Workshop.
Copyright © 1999 Sesame Street, Inc.

What are some kinds of plants?

You see them every day. Some tower over you. Some are smaller than your little finger. What are they? If you guessed plants, you were right!

There are many kinds of plants. Most plants have leaves. Some leaves are wide and flat. Others are as thin as needles. What kinds of leaves do you see in the picture?

Some plants have bright flowers. Some plants make fruits you can eat. Some grow best in hot, dry places. Others need lots of rain. What plants grow where you live?

Classify plants.

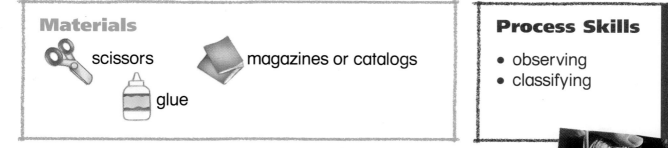

Materials

scissors

glue

magazines or catalogs

Process Skills

- observing
- classifying

Process Skills

Steps

1. Cut out pictures of plants from your magazines.

2. **Observe** the pictures. How are the plants alike? How are they different?

3. **Classify** the pictures in as many ways as you can.

Share. Glue your pictures on a chart to show one way you can **classify** plants.

Lesson Review

1. How do some plants look different from others?

2. Where do plants live?

3. **Tell** two ways you can classify plants.

What does a plant need to grow?

Pretend this window box is yours. What would you plant in it? How would you help your plants grow?

Plants need light to grow well. Some plants need a lot of sunlight. Others need only a little sunlight.

These plants grow in soil. They need air and water, too. With the right amounts of light, air, and water, most plants can grow well.

People can help plants grow. How is the boy in the picture helping his plants grow?

Make a light box.

Materials

 shoe box with lid

potted plant

Process Skills

- predicting
- observing

Process Skills

Steps

1. Make a light box like the one in the picture.

2. Cover the box with the lid. Place the box so the hole faces a sunny spot.

3. **Predict** how your plant will grow.

4. **Observe** your plant after one week.

Share. Draw how your plant grew in the box.

Lesson Review

1. What do plants need to help them grow?

2. How can people help plants grow?

3. **Tell** why your plant grew the way it did in the box.

Experiment with plants.

Process Skills

- experimenting
- predicting
- observing

Materials

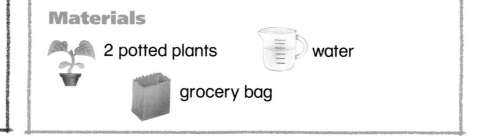

2 potted plants   water

grocery bag

Problem

What happens to plants that do not get light?

Give Your Hypothesis

If you put a plant in a dark place for a week, how will it look? Tell what you think.

Control the Variables

Make sure that both plants get the same amount of water.

Test Your Hypothesis

Follow these steps to do the **experiment**.

1 Water two plants.

2 Cover one plant with a bag. Put the other plant in the light.

3 **Predict.** How do you think the plants will look after one week?

4 **Observe** both plants after one week.

Collect Your Data

Use pictures like the ones shown. Draw your plants when you start. Draw your **prediction** for each plant. Draw what happened.

Tell Your Conclusion

Compare your results and hypothesis. What happens to plants that do not get light?

❓ Inquire Further

What would happen to the covered plant if you put it in a light place now?

Plant in light

When I started   My prediction   What happened

Covered plant

When I started   My prediction   What happened

Using Vocabulary Words

In your science book, you will see some words in dark print with yellow behind them. These words are vocabulary words. When you read the sentence, you will learn what the vocabulary word means. Here is an example.

The **stem** is the part of the plant that carries water to the leaves.

Stem is the vocabulary word. The rest of the sentence tells what **stem** means.

When you see vocabulary words in this book, write them in your science dictionary. Then write what they mean and draw a picture.

stem

—stem

stem

The stem is the part of the plant that carries water to the leaves.

Turn the page to learn some new vocabulary words.

Turn the page.

What are the parts of a plant?

A tree and a blade of grass do not look alike. Yet they both are plants. They both have the same parts.

What plant parts do you see in the picture? Find the plant's roots. The **roots** hold the plant in the soil. They also take in water from the soil.

stem

roots

The **stem** is the part of the plant that carries water to the leaves. The **leaves** use light, air, and water to make sugars that the plant needs to grow.

Many plants have flowers. **Flowers** make seeds. New plants grow from the seeds.

Lesson Review

1. What are the parts of a plant?

2. How do leaves use light, air, and water?

3. **Tell** what each part of a plant does.

leaves

flower

How does a plant grow and change?

Spring is here. The air is warm. Rain makes the soil soft and moist. Soon plants will start to grow.

tiny plant

stored food

Many plants grow from seeds. You can see a tiny plant inside this seed. The tiny plant uses the stored food as it grows.

Look at the picture of the growing plant. As the plant grows, the roots push down into the soil. Then the stem and leaves begin to grow.

Some plants make flowers too. The flowers will make seeds. Some of these seeds will grow into new plants. How will the new plants change as they grow?

Watch a plant grow.

Materials

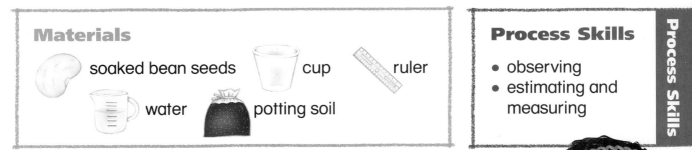

soaked bean seeds   cup   ruler

water   potting soil

Process Skills

- observing
- estimating and measuring

Steps

1. Put some potting soil in the cup.

2. Plant 2 or 3 seeds in the soil. Water the seeds.

3. Put your cup in a sunny spot.

4. **Observe** and draw what you see every 2 or 3 days.

5. **Measure** your plants once a week. Record.

Share. Compare your plants to a friend's plants.

Lesson Review

1. What is inside a seed?

2. How does a plant grow from a seed?

3. **Tell** how your plant has changed.

What is inside a seed?

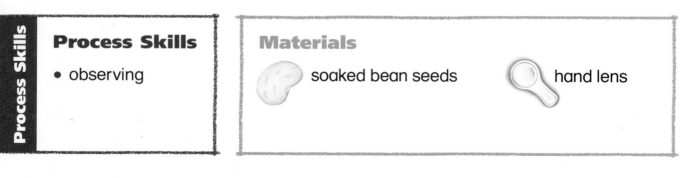

Process Skills

- observing

Materials

soaked bean seeds

hand lens

Steps

1. **Observe** your seed. Tell your partner what you see.

2. Split your seed into two parts with your fingernail.

3. Use a hand lens to **observe** the inside of the seed. Tell your partner what you see.

4. Draw a picture like this one. Label the tiny plant and the stored food.

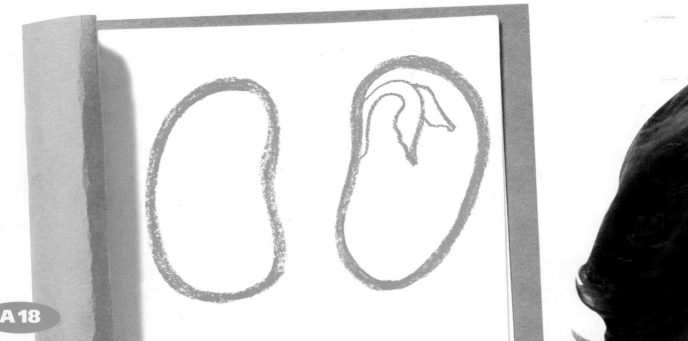

Think About Your Results

1. What are the parts of a seed?

2. How are the two halves of the seed different?

🔍 Inquire Further

How did the hand lens help you observe the seed? What in your classroom could you observe with a hand lens?

How are seeds scattered?

What is your favorite fruit? What kind of seeds does it have?

Fruits cover and protect seeds. The dandelion fruits in this picture have long feathery hairs that help them travel through the air. Find the fruits on this page that are shaped like wings. This shape helps them travel through the air.

When fruits travel, the seeds inside are scattered. **Scatter** means to spread out. Scattering helps carry seeds to new places where they can grow.

Have you ever found burrs like these stuck to your shoes or clothes? Burrs are fruits that travel by hooking onto people's clothing or animals' fur.

Seeds can travel in other ways too. Animals can eat fruits and drop the seeds to the ground. Some fruits or seeds float on the water to new places.

Lesson Review

1. What does scatter mean?

2. How do animals scatter seeds?

3. **Draw** some ways seeds are scattered.

How do people use plants?

Look around you. Do you see anything made from a plant? Many things you use every day come from plants!

▲ Look at this cotton plant. Many socks are made from cotton.

◀ Many kinds of bread are made from wheat.

▲ Maybe you have used aloe vera. Aloe is used in lotions and gels for the skin. It comes from an aloe plant.

◀ Trees give off oxygen. People need oxygen to stay alive.

Lesson Review

1. What food comes from wheat?

2. What is cotton used for?

3. **Write** some ways you use plants every day.

Chapter 1 Review

Reviewing Science Words

1. What do **roots** , **stems** , and **leaves** do?
2. What do **flowers** make?
3. Name three ways seeds are **scattered** .

Reviewing Science Ideas

1. Name things a plant needs to help it grow.
2. How do people use plants?

Make a flip book.

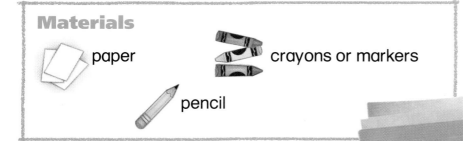

Materials

paper

crayons or markers

pencil

1 Have your teacher staple your papers along one edge.

2 Start on the first page. Draw a seed near the bottom edge of the paper.

3 On the next page, draw a seed just starting to grow.

4 Draw what the plant looks like as it grows. Make one drawing on each page.

5 Show your flip book to a friend. Flip the pages to see how a plant grows.

Chapter 2
Animals

You've Changed a Lot

🎵 Sing to the tune of *Froggy Went a Courtin'*.

Hey, little frog, you've changed a lot, ah hum.

You had a tail that was very long, ah hum.

You grew four legs as the tail disappeared.

Now you hop, hop, hop all through the year.

Ah hum, ah hum, ah hum.

Hey, butterfly, you've changed a lot, ah hum.

You started as a caterpillar, ah hum.

Then you lived inside a chrysalis.

You grew some wings, now you fly like this.

Ah hum, ah hum, ah hum.

Hey, little frog, you've changed a lot, ah hum.

Hey, butterfly, you've changed a lot, ah hum.

You're not the only ones that change.

Some are simple and some are strange!

Ah hum, ah hum, ah hum.

Original lyrics by Gerri Brioso and Richard Freitas.
Produced by Children's Television Workshop.

What are some kinds of animals?

Look outside. Do you see buildings or cars or sidewalks? Those are nonliving things. What living things do you see? Do you see birds, squirrels, or other animals?

There are different kinds of animals. **Mammals** are animals that have fur or hair. Birds have feathers. Most **reptiles** have dry, scaly skin. Fish have scales. **Amphibians** have moist, smooth skin.

Animals can live on land, in water, or in the air. They can even live in trees or under the ground. Where do the animals in these pictures live?

Guess the animal.

Materials

 paper

pencil or crayons

Process Skills

- communicating (ask, answer)

Process Skills

Steps

1. This is a game you can play with your class.

2. Draw an animal. Keep it a secret.

3. When it is your turn, the class will **ask** you questions about your animal. You can only **answer** yes or no.

4. If no one guesses your animal in ten questions, you win. Show the class your picture.

Share. Tell why you chose that animal.

Lesson Review

1. What is a mammal?

2. Name some places animals live.

3. **Show** how your animal moves by acting it out.

Ordering

These pictures are in order. Can you explain why?

1st

2nd

3rd

These pictures are not in order. Can you explain why?

How would you put these pictures in order?
Explain why.

Turn the page to find out how ordering can help you learn more about animals.

Turn the page.

How do frogs grow and change?

What baby animals have you seen? You may have seen kittens or puppies. Some animals look a lot like their parents.

Not all baby animals look like their parents. Some animals go through many changes as they grow. This is called the **life cycle**.

These pictures are in order. They show the life cycle of a frog. When a baby frog hatches from an egg, it is called a **tadpole**. A tadpole has a tail and no legs, and it swims and breathes in the water.

As the tadpole grows, its legs form. It becomes a full-grown frog. How does the frog look different from the tadpole?

Lesson Review

1. What is the life cycle?

2. What is a tadpole?

3. **Tell** how a frog changes as it grows. Talk about the changes in order.

How do butterflies grow and change?

You may have seen many different kinds of butterflies. Not all butterflies look alike, but they have the same life cycle. How do butterflies change as they grow?

Look at the picture of the egg. A caterpillar hatches from an egg. The caterpillar eats a lot and grows very quickly.

Then the caterpillar makes a covering called a **chrysalis**. Now the caterpillar is called a **pupa**.

Inside the chrysalis, the pupa begins to change. When it breaks out of the chrysalis, it is a butterfly!

Lesson Review

1. What is a chrysalis?

2. What is a pupa?

3. **Tell** how a butterfly changes as it grows.

How can you make a model of a butterfly life cycle?

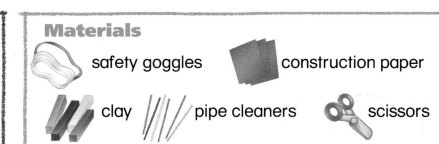

Process Skills

- making and using models

Materials

safety goggles

construction paper

clay

pipe cleaners

scissors

Steps

1. Put on your safety goggles.

2. Use clay to **make models** of an egg, a caterpillar, and a pupa in a chrysalis.

3. Now shape some clay into the body of a butterfly.

4. Add wings, legs, and antennae.

5. Use your **models** to show the life cycle of a butterfly.

Think About Your Results

1. What are the stages of a butterfly's life?

2. How does the butterfly change in each stage?

 Inquire Further

How else could you show the stages of
a butterfly's life?

Where do animals live?

Think about different animals you have seen. Where do these animals live?

A place where an animal lives is called its **habitat**. A habitat can be hot or cold or wet or dry. Animals get food, water, and shelter from their habitats. Many animals and plants become endangered when their habitats change. **Endangered** means that very few of these animals and plants are living.

What helps these animals live in their habitats? Webbed feet help a duck swim. A giraffe's long neck helps it reach leaves on tall trees. Seals have a thick layer of fat to help keep them warm. How does thick fur help seals live in their cold habitat?

Lesson Review

1. What is a habitat?

2. What helps a giraffe live in its habitat?

3. **Draw** a habitat and an animal that lives there.

What do animals eat?

Splash! The river otter dives into the water to catch a fish.

Animals need plants and other animals to stay alive. Some animals eat plants. Some animals eat other animals.

Plants use energy from the sun to make food. Animals eat the plants for food. Then other animals eat those animals. This is called the **food chain**. Talk about the food chain in this picture.

Make a model of a food chain.

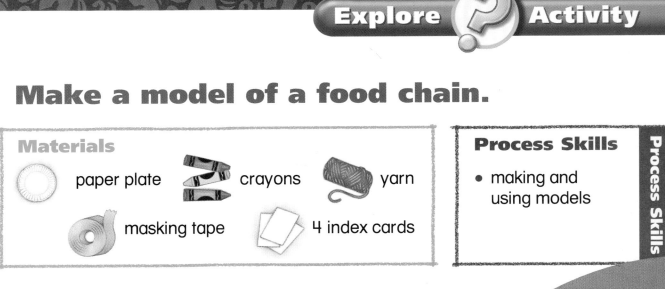

Materials

paper plate   crayons   yarn

masking tape   4 index cards

Process Skills

- making and using models

Process Skills

Steps

1. Color the plate yellow. This is the sun.

2. Draw these things, one on each card: a hawk, grass, a lizard, a bug.

3. Put the cards in order to **make a model** of a food chain.

4. Tape one end of the yarn to the back of the plate.

5. Tape the cards to the yarn in order.

Share. Tell about your food chain.

Lesson Review

1. What do animals eat?

2. What is the food chain?

3. **Tell** why the sun is important in a food chain.

How do animals protect themselves?

There is an animal in this picture!
Can you find it?

Some animals use color and shape to hide themselves. A color or shape that makes an animal hard to see is called **camouflage** .

Animals protect themselves in other ways too. Some animals can run quickly if they are being chased. Some animals have sharp teeth and claws for biting and scratching. Some animals have shells they can hide in. How does the animal in this picture protect itself?

Play a camouflage game.

Materials

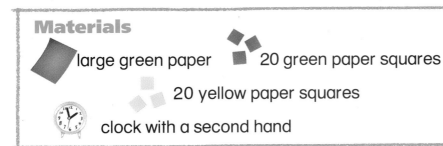

large green paper

20 green paper squares

20 yellow paper squares

clock with a second hand

Process Skills

- collecting and interpreting data

Process Skills

Steps

1 Take turns.

2 Have your partner put all of the squares on the large green paper.

3 Pick up as many squares as you can in ten seconds.

4 **Collect data** by counting how many squares of each color you picked up.

Share. Tell which color was easier to find and why.

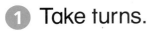

Lesson Review

1. What is camouflage?

2. What are some ways animals protect themselves?

3. **Tell** how camouflage can help an animal hide on a leaf.

Chapter 2 Review

Reviewing Science Words

1. How are **mammals** different from other animals?

2. What kind of skin do **reptiles** have?

3. What is the skin of an **amphibian** like?

4. How is a **tadpole** different from a frog?

5. Tell about a butterfly's **life cycle**. Talk about the **pupa** and the **chrysalis**.

6. What is a **habitat**?

7. Why do some plants and animals become **endangered**?

8. Why are plants an important part of the **food chain**?

9. How can **camouflage** help some animals?

Reviewing Science Ideas

1. What are some kinds of animals?

2. How do some animals protect themselves?

Make a poster.

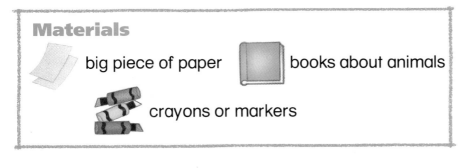

Materials

big piece of paper

books about animals

crayons or markers

① Work with a group.

② Read about animal habitats.

③ Choose a habitat.

④ Talk about which animals live in the habitat.

⑤ Draw the habitat and the animals on the big piece of paper.

Chapter 3
Fossils

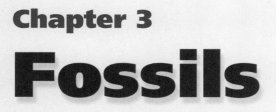

Sing to the tune of *Jingle Bells.*

A long long time ago
A leaf fell to the ground,
Got buried in some mud
And rock formed all around.

A long time after that
We dug deep underground
Looking for some clues
And guess what we have found.

Fossils here, fossils there,

Fossils far and near.

Fossils give us clues to things

That are no longer here.

Reading a Science Activity

Look at page A49. What is the title of the activity? The title can give you clues about what you will be doing.

Now look at the picture. How does the picture help you understand the activity?

What materials will you need? Get all the materials ready before you start.

Find the Process Skills box. This box tells you what science skills you will be using. Process Skill words are in **red.**

Read the steps. When you're ready to start, be sure to do the steps in order.

Draw a dinosaur.

Materials

paper   crayons   scissors

Process Skills

- observing

Process Skills

Steps

1. Draw a dinosaur and cut it out.

2. Look at your dinosaur.

3. Look at a friend's dinosaur.

4. **Observe** how they are alike and different.

Share. Tell about your dinosaur.

Turn the page to read a lesson and a science activity.

Turn the page.

What are fossils?

Think about animals that live in your neighborhood. You have probably seen dogs, cats, birds, and squirrels.

▲ trilobite

Other kinds of animals lived in the past. You can learn about them by studying fossils. **Fossils** are prints or remains of plants and animals that lived long ago.

Sometimes parts of plants or animals that have died get buried in mud. Over many years, the mud can turn to rock. The remains become fossils in the rock.

These fossils show how some plants and animals looked long ago. Which look like plants and animals that you have seen? Which look different?

▼ grasshopper

◄ fern

▲ snake

Make a leaf print.

Materials

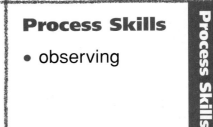

clay

leaves

Steps

1. Make your clay thin and flat.

2. Press a leaf into the clay.

3. Take the leaf out. **Observe** the print.

4. Put your leaf and print with other children's leaves and prints.

5. **Observe** each print. Try to match each print with its leaf.

Share. Compare your leaf print to other children's prints.

Lesson Review

1. What are fossils?

2. How do fossils form?

3. **Tell** how your print is like your leaf and how it is different.

How do we learn about dinosaurs?

Have you ever seen a living dinosaur? Of course not! Yet you probably have an idea of what some dinosaurs looked like. People have learned a lot about dinosaurs from fossils.

Fossils give clues about the past. You can find out what dinosaurs looked like by looking at fossils of their bones. Look at the skeleton of the Stegosaurus. The Stegosaurus had bony plates on its back and sharp spikes on its tail.

Stegosaurus

You can learn about what dinosaurs ate by looking at fossils of their teeth. The Centrosaurus apertus ate plants. It had a sharp beak for grabbing plants and leaves. It had short teeth for chewing plants. The Tyrannosaurus rex had long, sharp teeth for eating meat.

Centrosaurus apertus

Tyrannosaurus rex

Lesson Review

1. What can you learn about dinosaurs by looking at their fossils?

2. How did a beak help the Centrosaurus apertus eat plants?

3. **Tell** what you can learn about the Stegosaurus by looking at its bones.

What are some kinds of dinosaurs?

Did you know that there were hundreds of different kinds of dinosaurs? Some were small and fast. Others were very big and very heavy. How many dinosaurs can you name?

Compare the dinosaurs in the picture. Tyrannosaurus rex was the largest meat-eating animal that we know of. It was as long as a school bus and as tall as a small house.

Alamosaurus was as long as two school buses. It had a long neck for reaching tall plants.

Tyrannosaurus rex

Dromaeosaurus

Dromaeosaurus was about as long as your bed. It was a fast runner and hunted in groups.

Ankylosaurus was a plant eater. How do you think Ankylosaurus protected itself?

Lesson Review

1. How long was a Tyrannosaurus rex?

2. How did a long neck help the Alamosaurus?

3. **Tell** how two of the dinosaurs in the picture are different from each other.

Alamosaurus

Ankylosaurus

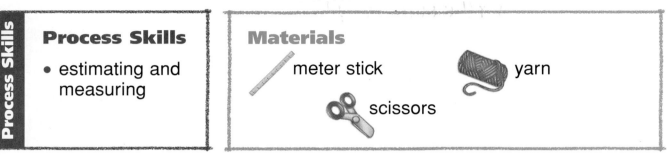
How long were some dinosaurs?

Process Skills

- estimating and measuring

Materials

meter stick

yarn

scissors

Steps

1. Choose a dinosaur from the chart.

2. Use a meter stick to **measure.**

3. Roll out your yarn until it is the length of your dinosaur.

4. Use your yarn to find something else that is about the same length as your dinosaur.

Dinosaur	Length
Ceratosaurus	6 meters
Megalosaurus	9 meters
Allosaurus	12 meters
Alamosaurus	21 meters
Brachiosaurus	23 meters
Diplodocus	26 meters

Dinosaur	
Length	
Object that is the same length	

Think About Your Results

1. What is about the same length as your dinosaur?

2. What would be about the same length as two dinosaurs?

Inquire Further

How else could you measure the length of a dinosaur?

What happened to the dinosaurs?

Dinosaurs lived on the earth for millions of years. Now only their fossils are left. What do you think happened to the dinosaurs?

Dinosaurs are extinct. An **extinct** animal is a kind of animal that no longer lives on the earth.

We can learn about extinct animals by studying the fossils they left behind. Scientists who study fossils are called **paleontologists**.

Scientists do not know for sure what happened to the dinosaurs. Some scientists believe that a meteor crashed into the earth. Dust from the meteor may have blocked the sunlight, causing plants to die. Without plants to eat, dinosaurs could not live.

Paleontologists are still learning about dinosaurs from the fossils they find.

Lesson Review

1. What does extinct mean?

2. What do paleontologists do?

3. **Tell** what some scientists believe happened to the dinosaurs.

Chapter 3 Review

Reviewing Science Words

1. What are **fossils**?

2. What might have caused the dinosaurs to become **extinct**?

3. How do **paleontologists** learn about dinosaurs?

Reviewing Science Ideas

1. How do fossils form?

2. How do we learn about dinosaurs?

3. Describe some different kinds of dinosaurs.

Make a clay dinosaur.

Materials

 clay

1 Choose a dinosaur.

2 Make a model of your dinosaur out of clay.

3 Tell about your dinosaur. Talk about its size and what it ate.

Unit A
Performance Review

You have learned a lot about plants and animals. You have learned about dinosaurs too. Think of something you would like to show your classmates. Have a game day!

Plan your game day.

1. Pick a project you would like to do.

2. Find the things you will need to do your project.

3. Think about how to present your project so others will understand.

Make a puzzle.

Draw a picture of a plant or animal on heavy paper. Cut your picture into pieces to make a puzzle. Give your puzzle to a partner to put together. Tell your partner about your picture.

Put on a skit.

Act out one thing you learned. You can use props to help. Have your skit tell a story. You can work with a partner.

Play a game.

With a partner, write words about plants and animals on cards. Turn the cards over. Make a spinner. Take turns spinning the spinner and turning over a card. If the word on the card and the word on the spinner go together, keep the card. If they do not, turn the card over. Play until all the cards are taken.

Writing about a Plant, Animal, or Dinosaur

Before you write a description, you need to choose a topic. Then think about words that describe your topic. When you describe something, you can tell how it looks, sounds, feels, smells, or tastes.

1. **Prewrite** Talk with your partner about things you can write about. Choose a plant, animal, or dinosaur. Draw a picture of it.

2. **Draft** Write sentences about your picture.

3. **Revise** Read what you wrote. Do you like it? Make changes if you want to.

4. **Edit** Check your writing to make sure it is correct. Make a neat copy.

5. **Publish** Share your picture and your writing with others. You can make a booklet or find another way to share.

Unit B
Physical Science

Science and Technology
In Your World!

What makes this balloon go up?

First the balloon is filled with cold air. Then the air is heated. Hot air is lighter than the air around it. So the balloon is able to float.

Chapter 1
Matter

These lollipops have special lines on them.

When light hits the lines, the light bends and bounces. The way the light moves makes the pictures of dinosaurs appear.

Chapter 2
Sound, Heat, and Light

A special machine uses electricity to make sharks swim away.

Some divers use these machines when they go in deep water. These machines may soon be put on surfboards and life jackets too.

Chapter 3
Force, Magnets, and Electricity

Chapter 1
Matter

♪ Sing to the tune of *Skip to My Lou.*

There's water in the pitcher, ready to pour.

There's water in the pitcher, ready to pour.

Pour it in the ice trays we bought at the store.

Then put them in the freezer.

Wait a little while, then take them out.

The water has changed, what's this about?

It turned into ice, without a doubt.

What can we make with ice cubes?

Put the ice in the glass and go to the store.

Buy some lemons, you know what they're for.

But when you come back, there's no ice anymore.

All you have is water.

Original lyrics by Gerri Brioso and Richard Freitas.
Produced by Children's Television Workshop.

B5

Sorting

When you put objects into groups, you are sorting. These blocks are sorted by color.

These blocks are sorted by shape. Find another way to sort the blocks.

Turn the page to find out how sorting can help you learn about objects.

Turn the page.

What are the properties of objects?

Find a toy in the picture that is green, round, and bounces. Which toy is it?

You're right! The ball is green, round, and bounces. You used the ball's properties to tell it apart from the other toys.

Some **properties** of objects are color, shape, and size. How much an object weighs and how it feels are other properties.

Find the sailboat. Do you think it floats? Whether an object floats or sinks is a property. What are some other properties of the sailboat?

Sort objects.

Materials

common classroom objects

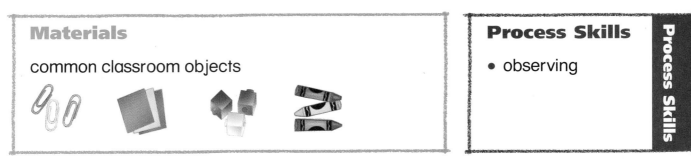

Process Skills

- observing

Process Skills

Steps

1. Gather some objects from your classroom.

2. **Observe** the objects. Describe them to a friend.

3. Sort your objects by color.

4. Now sort your objects by shape.

5. Find another way to sort your objects.

Share. Find as many ways to sort your objects as you can. Tell a friend about some of the ways you found.

Lesson Review

1. What are some properties of the ball in the picture?

2. What are some properties of objects?

3. **Tell** four ways you can sort objects.

What is matter?

Can you find the football on the bed and the shoes on the floor? What else do you see in this bedroom?

Everything in this room is made of matter. In fact, everything around you is made of matter.

Matter is anything that takes up space and has weight. What do you see in your classroom that is made of matter?

Some things that you cannot see are made of matter. Even the air around you is matter.

Compare objects.

Materials

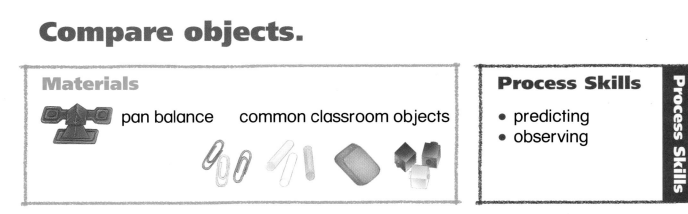

pan balance   common classroom objects

Process Skills

- predicting
- observing

Steps

1. How would you put your objects in order from lightest to heaviest? **Predict.**

2. Put one object in each pan. **Observe.**

3. Compare the weight of each object.

4. Put the objects in order from lightest to heaviest. Record.

Share. Compare your results with your prediction.

Lesson Review

1. What is matter?

2. What are some things that are made of matter?

3. **Tell** how a balance can help you learn about matter.

What are the states of matter?

Look up! Look down! Look all around! What do you see?

You know that everything around you is made of matter. There are three states of matter. The **states of matter** are solids, liquids, and gases.

A **solid** has a size and shape of its own. Which things in the picture are solids?

A **liquid** takes the shape of its container. Paint is a liquid. What other liquids do you know about?

A **gas** can change shape and size. When you fill a balloon with gas, the gas takes the shape and size of the balloon. You know that air is all around you. Air is made of gases you cannot see.

Lesson Review

1. What is a solid?
2. What is a liquid?
3. **Write** a list of some solids, liquids, and gases.

How can matter be mixed?

Help your family make dinner. Toss the salad. Stir the lemonade. As you cook, you are mixing different kinds of matter.

What would you put in a salad? You might put in some lettuce, carrots, and tomatoes. When you toss the salad, you are mixing solids together.

How could you make a dressing for the salad? You might mix oil and vinegar together. Then, you are mixing two liquids.

Look at the lemonade in the picture. It is made of a solid mixed with a liquid.

Look around you. What things do you see in your classroom that are mixed together?

Find out what mixes with water.

Materials

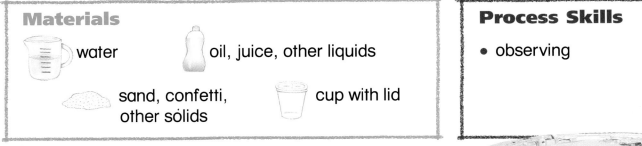

water

oil, juice, other liquids

sand, confetti, other solids

cup with lid

Process Skills

- observing

Process Skills

Steps

1. Put some water in a cup.

2. Add one of the solids or liquids.

3. Put the lid on the cup and shake the cup gently.

4. Put the cup down. **Observe.**

5. Wait 2 minutes. **Observe** again.

6. Do the activity again with a different material.

Share. Tell how your materials mixed with water.

Lesson Review

1. Name two solids that can be mixed.

2. Name a solid that can be mixed with a liquid.

3. **Write** two ways that different materials can mix with water.

How can matter be changed?

When you mold clay into different shapes, you are changing the way matter looks.

Matter can be changed in many ways. It can change from one state to another. When matter is heated, it can melt. When something melts, it changes from a solid to a liquid. Find something in the picture that is melting.

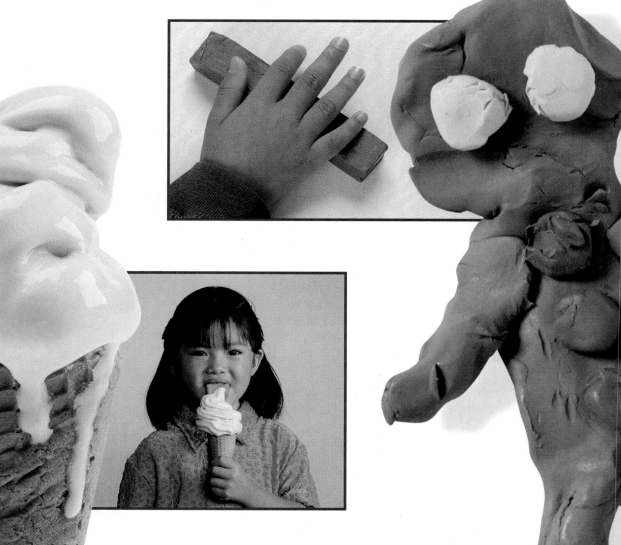

Matter can be cooled until it freezes. Then it changes from a liquid to a solid. Find something in the picture that is frozen.

What are some other ways to change matter?

Lesson Review

1. What happens when an object melts?
2. What happens when an object freezes?
3. **Tell** three ways to change matter.

How fast can you melt an ice cube?

Process Skills

Process Skills

- predicting
- observing

Materials

ice cube

plate

clock

Steps

1 Put your ice cube on your plate.

2 How can you make your ice cube melt fast? Write down your ideas. Pick one way to try.

3 **Predict** how long it will take you to melt your ice cube.

4 Record the starting time.

5 **Observe** your ice cube as it melts.

6 How long did it take you to melt your ice cube? Record the ending time.

7 Compare your results with your **prediction**.

Think About Your Results

1. What did you do to melt your ice cube?

2. What was the fastest way someone in your class melted his or her ice cube?

Inquire Further

What would be a fast way to melt a large block of ice?

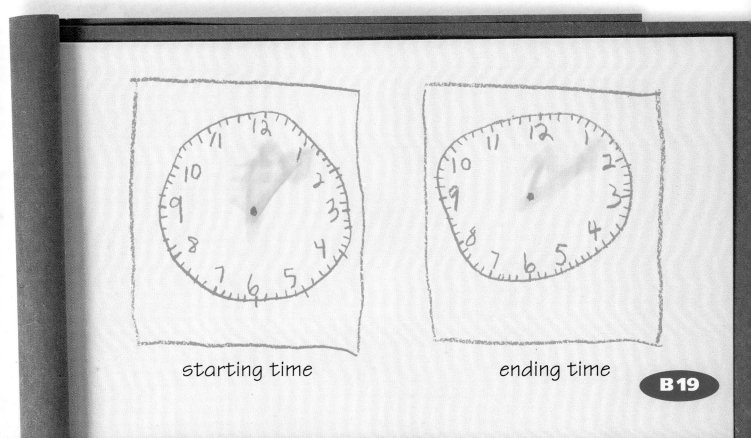

starting time   ending time

Chapter 1 Review

Reviewing Science Words

1. What are some **properties** of a ball?

2. What is **matter** ?

3. What are the **states of matter** ?

4. List some things that are **solids** .

5. What happens to a **liquid** when you pour it into a different container?

6. What happens to the shape of a **gas** when you fill a balloon?

Reviewing Science Ideas

1. Give an example of two kinds of matter mixed together.

2. How can heat change matter?

Play a guessing game.

Materials

paper

pencil

1. Think of an object. Keep it a secret.

2. Write down clues about your object.
   Your clues should include some properties
   of your object and its state of matter.

3. Read your clues aloud. Give your group
   ten tries to guess your object.

Sound, Heat, and Light

They're All Around

♪ Sing to the tune of *Three Blind Mice*.

Chorus

Heat, light, sound.

Heat, light, sound.

They're all around.

They're all around.

What could you do to make some heat?

Try rubbing your hands as you hear the beat.

Then touch your face, you can feel the heat.

Sing the chorus.

When you block the light what comes into view?

It's something different, it's something new.

It's a special shadow made just by you.

Sing the chorus.

What are some ways you can make a sound?

Tap a glass with a spoon, give a pillow a pound.

Or pluck a string and you'll hear a sound.

Sing the chorus.

Original lyrics by Gerri Brioso and Richard Freitas.
Produced by Children's Television Workshop.

How can you make sounds?

Bang! Whir! What made those sounds? A balloon popped. Someone blew a noisemaker. What a noisy party!

There are many ways to make sounds. Sound is made when an object vibrates. **Vibrate** means to move back and forth. What objects in the picture vibrate to make sound?

Volume is how loud or soft a sound is. What loud and soft sounds have you heard?

Talk about the picture. What other sounds would you hear at a party? How would you describe these sounds?

Make sounds.

Materials

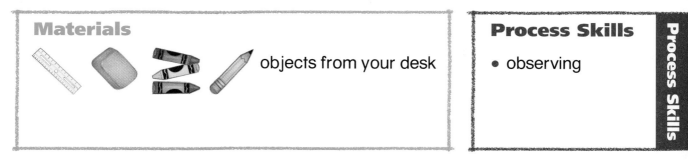 objects from your desk

Process Skills

• observing

Process Skills

Steps

1 Have your partner cover his or her eyes.

2 Use objects from your desk to make a sound. Ask your partner to **observe** by listening.

3 Have your partner guess how you made the sound.

4 Take turns.

Share. Draw some ways to make sounds.

Lesson Review

1. How are sounds made?

2. What is volume?

3. **Tell** how you can change the volume of a sound.

What is pitch?

Sing a song! Hum a tune! Listen to your voice go up and down.

Sounds can be high or low. **Pitch** is how high or low a sound is. What high and low sounds have you heard?

The pitch of a sound can be changed. It can become higher or lower. When you sing, you change the pitch of your voice.

Talk about the sounds these instruments make. How could you change the pitch of each instrument?

Make a pitch finder.

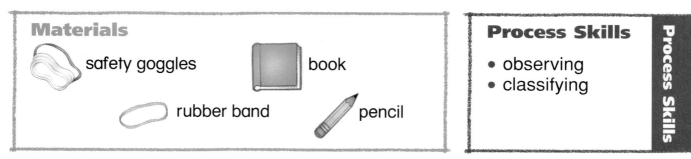

Materials

safety goggles

book

rubber band

pencil

Process Skills

- observing
- classifying

Process Skills

Steps

1 Put on your safety goggles. Make a pitch finder like the one in the picture.

2 Hold the pencil in place. Pluck the rubber band. **Observe** the sound.

3 Find ways to change the sound. **Classify** each sound as high or low.

Share. Draw your pitch finder. Show how you made high and low sounds.

Lesson Review

1. What is pitch?

2. How did you change the pitch?

3. **Show** how you can make high and low sounds.

What are some sources of heat?

It is a hot day! Heat comes from the light of the sun. Heat comes from other places too.

Sunlight is a source of heat. A **source** is a place from which something comes. Rubbing things together can produce heat. What heat sources are in the picture? What other heat sources do you know about?

You can use heat to cook. Heat moves from warmer places and objects to cooler ones. It moves from the hot fire to the cold food.

Heat moves easily through metal. It does not move easily through wood and cloth. How do the people in the picture protect their hands from the heat?

Lesson Review

1. What is a source?

2. What are some sources of heat?

3. **Draw** a picture of food being cooked on a stove. Draw an arrow to show which way the heat moves.

Which container will warm up fastest?

Process Skills

- observing
- predicting

Materials

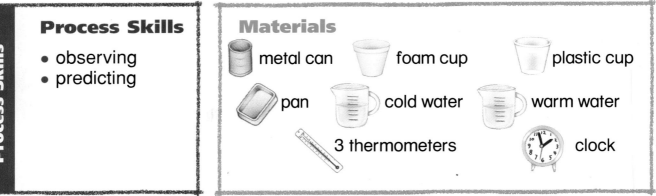

metal can   foam cup   plastic cup

pan   cold water   warm water

3 thermometers   clock

Steps

1. Put cold water and a thermometer in each container.

2. **Observe** each thermometer.

3. Use pictures like the ones shown. Mark the temperature on each picture.

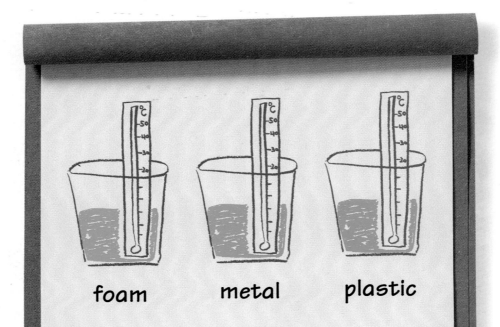

foam   metal   plastic

④ Set the containers in a pan of warm water.

⑤ Which container will warm up fastest? **Predict.**

⑥ Wait 5 minutes. **Observe** and mark each temperature again.

⑦ Which container warmed up fastest? Compare your results with your **prediction.**

Think About Your Results

1. Which container warmed up fastest?

2. Does heat move more easily through metal, plastic, or foam? Explain.

Inquire Further

Suppose you wanted to keep ice cubes from melting. What kind of container would you use? Why?

What are some sources of light?

Think about your room at night. What is it like? You probably cannot see very well. You need light in order to see.

Light comes from the sun, fire, and light bulbs. Most light sources also give off heat. What other light sources do you know about?

Talk about these pictures. How are they alike and different? What sources of light do you see?

What does light look like to you? You might be surprised to learn that white light is really made up of many colors.

Sometimes you can see the colors in light after a rainstorm. When sunlight moves through drops of water in the air, the light is separated into the colors of a rainbow. These colors are red, orange, yellow, green, blue, indigo, and violet. What colors do you see in this rainbow?

Lesson Review

1. What are some sources of light?

2. How does a rainbow form?

3. **Draw** a rainbow.

B 33

Using a Word Web

This is a word web. You can use a word web to group your ideas. Point to the topic. The topic is what the word web is about. Point to the examples. Each example tells something about the topic.

This word web has been started.
What is the topic? What are the examples?
How would you complete the word web?

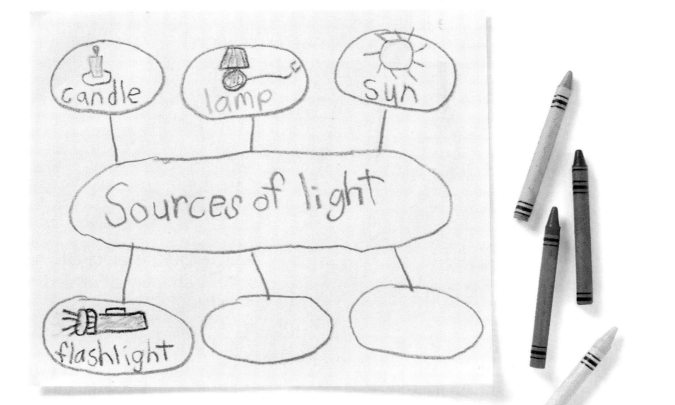

Turn the page to find out how a word
web can help you learn more about light.

Turn the
page.

How does light move?

Can you walk in a straight line? Can you walk in a zigzag? How many other ways can you move? Did you know that light moves too?

Light moves in straight lines. This word web shows what happens when light hits different objects.

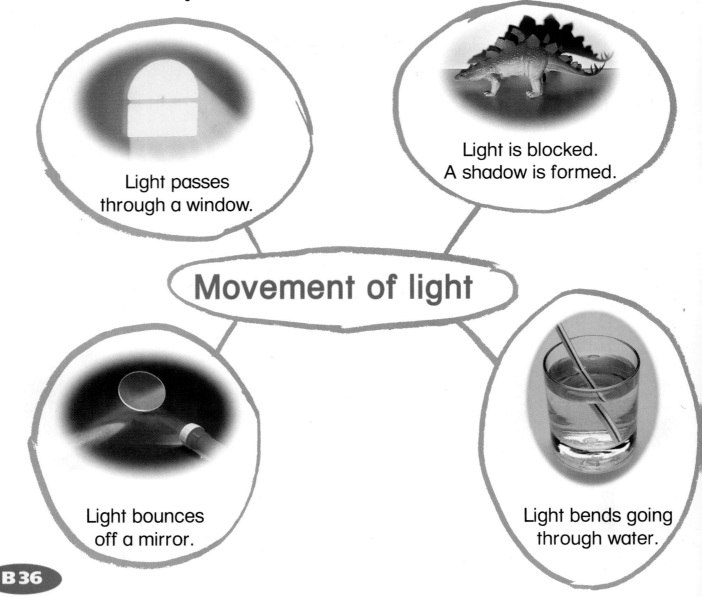

Light passes through a window.

Light is blocked. A shadow is formed.

Movement of light

Light bounces off a mirror.

Light bends going through water.

Go on a scavenger hunt.

Materials

 flashlight

Process Skills
- observing

Process Skills

Steps

1. Use your flashlight. Find one object in the room that makes light bounce.

2. Find one object that makes light bend.

3. Find one object that light can pass through.

4. Find one object that blocks light.

Share. Make a word web. Draw or write the name of each object you **observed**.

Lesson Review

1. How does light move?

2. What happens when light hits a mirror?

3. **Show** an object that blocks light.

Experiment with shadows.

Process Skills

- experimenting
- observing

Materials

flashlight   toy or
classroom object

Problem

How can you change the size of a shadow?

Give Your Hypothesis

If you move an object farther from a light,
will the shadow get larger or smaller? Tell what
you think.

Control the Variables

Make sure you keep your flashlight steady.

Test Your Hypothesis

Follow these steps to do the **experiment**.

1. Shine the flashlight on a wall.

2. Put the object close to the light.
   Observe the shadow.

3. Now put the object far from the light.
   Observe the shadow again.

Collect Your Data

Use a chart like this one. Draw pictures to show the size of each shadow.

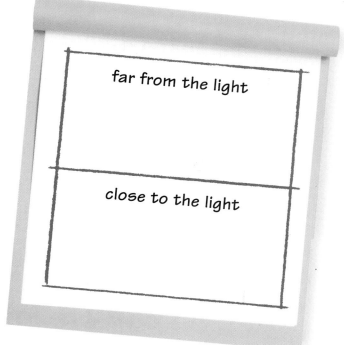

far from the light

close to the light

Tell Your Conclusion

Compare your results and hypothesis. How can you change the size of a shadow?

? Inquire Further

In what other ways can you change the shadow?

Chapter 2 Review

Reviewing Science Words

1. What are some things that can change **volume**?

2. What are some things that can change **pitch**?

3. How can you make an object **vibrate**?

4. What **sources** of light do you see in the room?

Reviewing Science Ideas

1. How are sounds made?

2. Name two sources of heat.

3. Does heat move more easily through metal or wood?

4. How does a shadow form?

Make a collage.

Materials

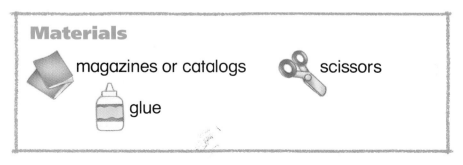

magazines or catalogs

glue

scissors

① Work with a group.

② Find pictures that show sound, heat, and light.

③ Tell about your pictures.

④ Glue your pictures onto a collage.

Chapter 3

Force, Magnets, and Electricity

♪ Sing to the tune of *Pop Goes the Weasel*.

You have a train, but it won't run,
Because you need a battery.
But there's another way to go.
Try using gravity.

Hold the train at the top of a hill.
Then take your hand away.
Watch it rolling all the way down.
Gravity saved the day!

You know you have a metal train.
So guess what you can do.
Put a magnet very close by.
It pulls the train to you!

Then you find a battery.
You quickly put it in.
Flick the switch, the train takes off.
And does a little spin!

Cause and Effect

Talk about the picture.

A **cause** is what makes something happen.
The **effect** is what happens.

The boy is going to kick the ball. What will the
effect be?

The popcorn spilled. What was the cause?

Turn the page to learn what causes objects to move.

Turn the page.

What makes objects move?

Whoosh! Crack! The ball flies through the air. What caused the ball to move?

The batter caused the ball to move. An object moves when it is pushed or pulled. **Force** is the push or pull that makes something move. The more force you use, the more the object moves.

You can use force to move an object up, down, right, or left. You can make it move in a straight line, a curve, or even a zigzag. How do you use force to move objects every day?

Make an object move.

Materials

ruler   common classroom objects

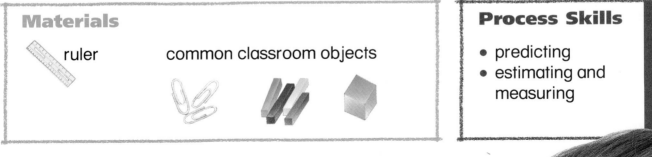

Process Skills

- predicting
- estimating and measuring

Process Skills

Steps

1. Choose one object.

2. If you blow on it, how far will it go? **Predict.**

3. Blow on your object. **Measure** how far it goes.

4. How can you make it go farther?

5. Choose a new object. Do the activity again.

Share. Compare your results with a friend's results.

Lesson Review

1. What is force?

2. When you use a lot of force to move an object, what happens?

3. **Tell** how you can make an object move.

What is gravity?

It is a fun day at the park! What force is making the boy slide down the slide?

The boy slides down because of gravity. **Gravity** is the force that pulls things down.

When you jump into the air, gravity pulls you back down. If you let go of an object, gravity makes it fall. If you lose your balance, you will fall too.

Explore gravity.

Materials

common classroom objects

- predicting

Steps

1. If you drop two objects at the same time, which will hit the floor first? **Predict.**

2. Hold two objects at the same height and drop them at the same time.

3. Which hit the floor first?

4. Try it again with two new objects.

Share. Compare your predictions with your results.

Lesson Review

1. What is gravity?

2. What happens if you let go of an object?

3. **Show** what happens when you drop two objects from the same height at the same time.

What is a magnet?

Have you ever seen objects stick to a rock? Certain metal objects will stick to a rock called a lodestone. Lodestone is a natural magnet.

lodestone

Magnets can push or pull certain metal objects. A **pole** is the place on a magnet that has the strongest push or pull.

Find the north and south poles on the magnets in the picture. Opposite poles attract each other. **Attract** means to pull toward. Like poles repel each other. **Repel** means to push away.

What do you think would happen if two south poles were put together?

Push and pull magnets.

Materials

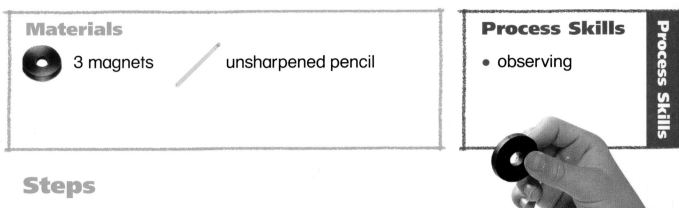

3 magnets   unsharpened pencil

Process Skills

- observing

Steps

1. Hold your pencil like the one in the picture.

2. Put a magnet onto your pencil.

3. Put another magnet on the pencil. **Observe.**

4. Flip the top magnet over. **Observe.**

5. Put a third magnet on the pencil. **Observe.**

Share. Draw your pencil. Show how it looks before you flip the top magnet over and then after you flip the magnet.

Lesson Review

1. What does a magnet do?

2. What happens when opposite poles of two magnets are put together?

3. **Tell** what happens when you flip the top magnet over. Explain why.

What can a magnet attract?

Wow! This big magnet looks strong! Can it pull all these things toward it? What can a magnet attract?

A magnet attracts certain metal objects. You can use a magnet to find out which kinds of metal objects it will attract.

Talk about the objects in the picture. Which ones do you think the magnet will attract? Why?

Go fishing with a magnet.

Materials

 magnet

unsharpened pencil

string

common classroom objects

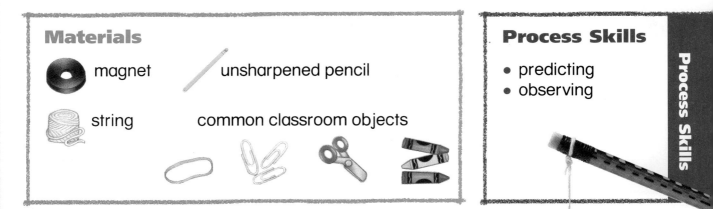

Steps

1 Tie one end of your string to a magnet.

2 Tie the other end to a pencil.

3 Which objects will your magnet attract? **Predict.**

4 Dip your magnet into a group of objects.

5 Which objects does your magnet attract? **Observe.**

Share. Make a list of objects a magnet will attract.

Lesson Review

1. What does a magnet attract?

2. Name some things a magnet does not attract.

3. **Tell** how you can predict whether a magnet will attract an object.

How many paper clips will a magnet pick up?

Process Skills

- predicting
- observing

Materials

magnet   paper clips

Steps

1. Use a chart like the one in the picture.

2. How many paper clips will your magnet pick up? Record your **prediction** by coloring in the chart.

3. Put your magnet into a pile of paper clips.

4. Lift the magnet out. **Observe.**

5. How many paper clips did your magnet pick up? Record your results.

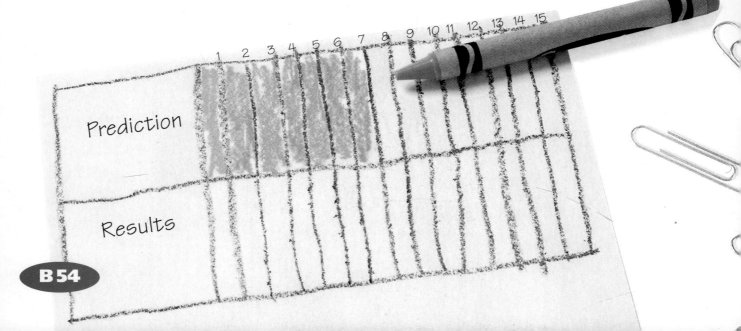

Think About Your Results

1. How many paper clips did your magnet pick up?

2. When one paper clip was picked up, what happened to the paper clips near it?

Inquire Further

How would your magnet need to change to pick up more paper clips?

How does electricity move?

Turn on a light. What happens? Electricity makes the light work.

Electricity travels in a path called a **circuit**. If you want to turn on a light, a complete circuit must be made.

Electricity can be stored in a battery. Look at the pictures. Which bulb is lit? Why?

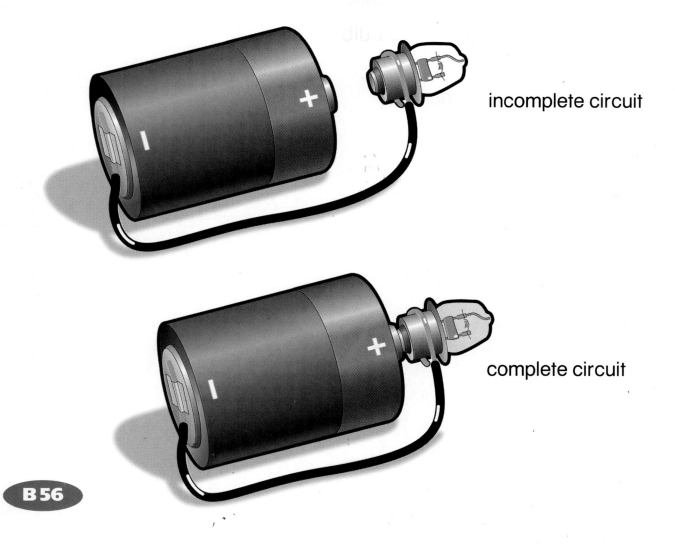

incomplete circuit

complete circuit

Light a bulb.

Materials

safety goggles

wire

light bulb

battery

Process Skills

- observing

Steps

1. Put on your safety goggles.

2. Put your materials together to make a complete circuit.

3. How can you make the bulb light up? Observe.

Share. Tell how to make a complete circuit.

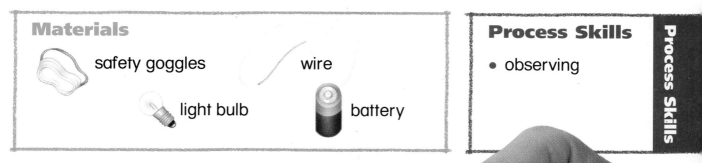

Lesson Review

1. What is a circuit?

2. Where can electricity be stored?

3. **Show** how you lit your bulb.

B 57

How do you use electricity safely?

Listen to music. Look at books. Work on the computer. There is so much to do at the library!

Electricity makes many things at the library work. It makes the lights work, so you can see and read. It makes the CD player work, so you can listen to music or stories.

What things in your school use electricity? What things at home use electricity?

You need to be careful when you use electricity. Do not touch wires or electrical outlets. Do not use anything with a broken cord or wire. Use electricity only in a dry place and keep your hands dry.

Lesson Review

1. What are some ways you use electricity?

2. Name some ways to stay safe when you are using electricity.

3. **Draw** an object that uses electricity.

Chapter 3 Review

Reviewing Science Words

1. How can you use **force** to make an object move?

2. What does **gravity** do?

3. If two **poles** that are alike come together, do they **attract** or **repel** each other?

4. What is a **circuit**?

Reviewing Science Ideas

1. What are some ways objects can move?

2. Name three things a magnet will attract.

3. How does electricity move?

4. How can you use electricity safely?

Build a toy that moves.

Materials

 magnets   common classroom objects

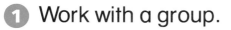

① Work with a group.

② Design a toy.

③ Talk about different ways you can make your toy move.

④ Build your toy and decorate it.

Unit B
Performance Review

How can you show what you have learned about force? You can write, draw, or act things out. Choose one thing to show your friends. Have a festival to show what you have learned.

Plan your festival.

1. Pick a project you would like to do.

2. Get what you need for your project.

3. Plan how to show your project to others.

Design a playground ride.

Think about things you see in a playground. Use what you know about force, magnets, and electricity to design a ride for your playground. Draw a picture of your ride. Make a class playground. Glue your picture along with classmates' pictures on a large sheet of paper. Take turns telling about your rides.

Make a chart.

Make a chart with three columns. Label the columns solids, liquids, and gases. Write words or draw pictures in the columns to show solids, liquids, or gases.

Write a song.

Write a song about sound, light, or heat. Make part of your song soft. Make part of your song loud. Use high and low sounds. Give your song a name and sing it to the class.

Writing Directions

When you explain how to do something, you are giving directions. You can draw pictures and write sentences to give directions for how to make something. Be sure to put the steps in the right order.

1. **Prewrite** Think of a noisemaker. Draw a picture of it.

2. **Draft** List the materials you want to use. Write the steps to make a noisemaker.

3. **Revise** Read the steps. Do they make sense? Read the list of materials. Did you forget anything? Make changes if you need to.

4. **Edit** Check your writing to make sure it is correct. Make a neat copy.

5. **Publish** Show your picture and directions to others. Now they can make the noisemaker.

Unit C
Earth Science

Science and Technology In Your World!

What happens during an earthquake?

An earthquake simulator is a special shaking table. It can help scientists learn more about earthquakes. People can use this information to design buildings and bridges that are safer.

Chapter 1
The Earth

What does a weather satellite do?

It takes pictures that help scientists learn about clouds, temperature, and amounts of water in the air. The pictures help scientists predict the weather.

Chapter 2
Weather and Seasons

When do astronauts wear jetpacks?

They wear them when they step outside the space shuttle. Jetpacks help astronauts stay close to the shuttle when they work in space.

Chapter 3
The Solar System

The Earth

Mountains and Rocks

♪ Sing to the tune of *Frére Jacques*.

There's a mountain.

There's a mountain.

Here's a rock.

Here's a rock.

The rock came from the mountain.

The rock came from the mountain.

How is that?

How is that?

There's a river,
By the mountain.
Rushing by,
Rushing by.
Wearing down the mountain,
Breaking off some pieces.
Making rocks.
Making rocks.

Just like mountains,
Just like mountains,
Rocks change too.
Rocks change too.
Wind and water change their
Size and shape and texture.
Day by day.
Day by day.

Original lyrics by Gerri Brioso and Richard Freitas.
Produced by Children's Television Workshop.

What are some features of the earth?

What will you see if you look down from an airplane or a very high hill? You will probably see land and water.

The earth has mountains, hills, and valleys. It also has oceans, rivers, and lakes. These are all called features of the earth.

Ocean water is salty. Lakes, ponds, rivers, and streams are filled with fresh water.

What features of the earth can you see in this picture?

Make a model of features of the earth.

Materials

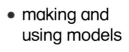 clay   sand   rocks

blue construction paper

Process Skills

- making and using models

Steps

1 Use your clay to **make a model** of land. Include hills, mountains, and valleys.

2 Add sand and rocks to your **model**.

3 Use blue paper to show water.

Share. Name the features of the earth shown in your **model**.

Lesson Review

1. What are some features of the earth?

2. Where can you find fresh water?

3. **Draw** a picture of some features of the earth.

Using Descriptive Words

You use descriptive words to tell about objects. Descriptive words tell about an object's properties. They tell about an object's color, shape, size, and texture.

Describe one of the objects in each section.

Color

Shape

Size

Texture

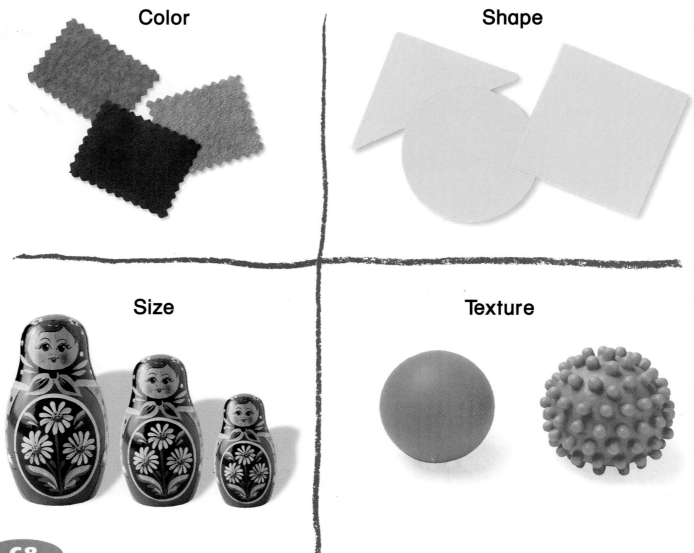

Read each of these sentences.
Can you picture this object?

1. It is a rectangle.

2. It is a rectangle. It is red, white, and blue.

3. It is a rectangle. It is red, white, and blue.
It has stars and stripes.

4. It is a rectangle. It is red, white, and blue.
It has stars and stripes. You might see it
hanging from a pole.

Draw the object.

Which descriptive words helped you
the most? Why?

Turn the page to find out how you can use
descriptive words to tell about rocks.

Turn the
page.

What are rocks like?

What a beautiful rock collection! How would you describe the rocks in this picture?

Rocks come in many sizes, shapes, and colors. Some rocks are shiny and smooth. Others are dull and rough. Some rocks are small enough to fit in your hand. Others are as big as a tree.

Rocks are made of minerals. If you look closely at some of these rocks, you might see different colors. Each color is a mineral that is part of the rock.

Lesson Review

1. What are rocks made of?

2. How can rocks be different from each other?

3. **Write** about one of the rocks in the picture. Use descriptive words.

How can rocks and soil be changed?

Can you find the path in this picture? The path was made by water. What happened to the soil that used to be there?

The soil may have been slowly washed away by the water. The soil may also have been worn away by small pieces of rock that were carried in the water.

When soil or rock are carried away by water, wind, or other rocks, it is called **erosion**. Plant roots help prevent erosion by keeping the soil in place.

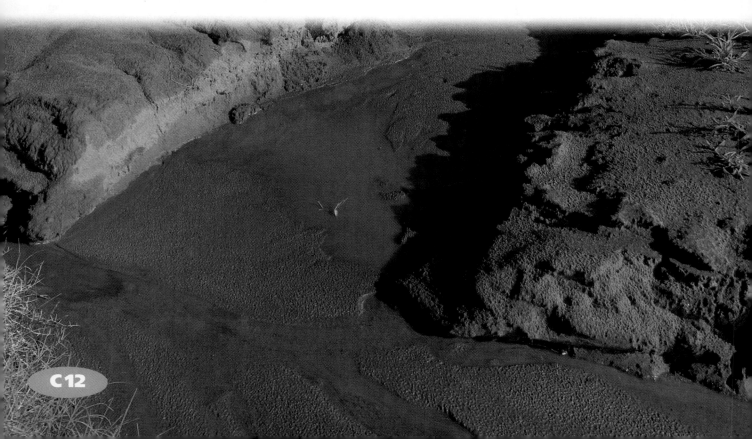

Show erosion.

Materials

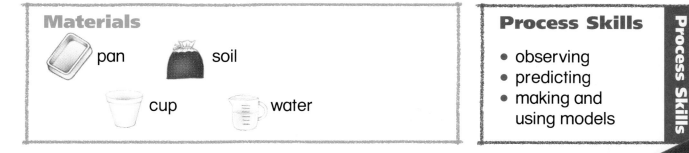

pan   soil   cup   water

Process Skills

- observing
- predicting
- making and using models

Steps

1. Put some soil in your pan. **Make a model** of a mountain.

2. **Predict** what will happen if you pour water onto the soil.

3. Hold the cup over the soil.

4. Have a partner slowly pour some water into the cup. **Observe.**

Share. Tell how you showed erosion.

Lesson Review

1. What is erosion?

2. How do plants help the soil?

3. **Draw** your soil before and after you poured the water.

How do volcanoes and earthquakes change the earth?

Fountains of red-hot liquid squirt high into the air. This volcano is erupting!

When a volcano erupts, lava is pushed out. **Lava** is melted rock that comes from inside the earth. Hot lava that flows from a volcano can hurt people and animals and harm the land.

When lava cools, it hardens into solid rock. Over time, the cooled lava can build up into a mountain.

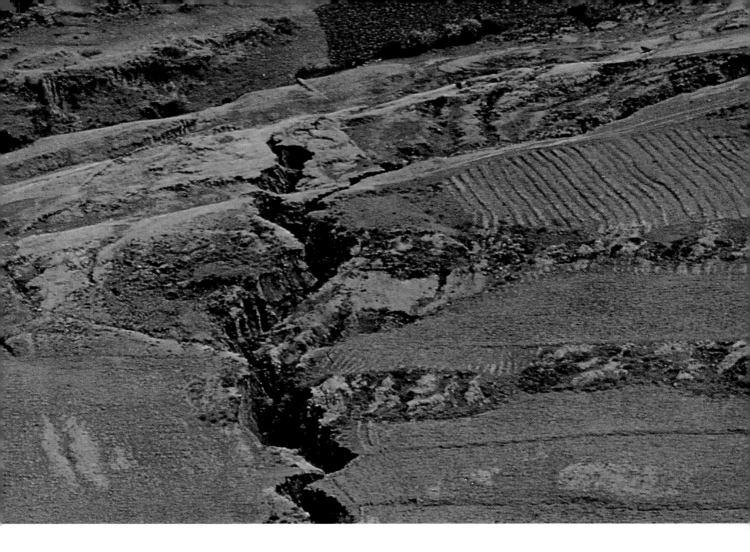

When an earthquake happens, the earth shakes back and forth. Roads, bridges, and buildings can be ruined.

An earthquake can change the land quickly. How did an earthquake change the land in this picture?

Lesson Review

1. What is lava?

2. What happens when a volcano erupts?

3. **Tell** how volcanoes and earthquakes change the earth.

How can you make a model of a volcano?

Process Skills

- making and using models
- estimating and measuring
- observing

Materials

safety goggles   clay   container

pan   teaspoon   craft stick

dishwashing soap   baking soda

vinegar   red food coloring

Steps

1 Put on your safety goggles.

2 **Make a model.** Mold the clay around the container in the shape of a volcano. Put your model in the pan.

3 **Measure.** Put 3 teaspoons of baking soda into the container. Add 2 teaspoons of dishwashing soap. Stir with the craft stick.

4 Add red food coloring.

5 Fill the rest of the container with vinegar.

6 Observe.

Think About Your Results

1. How is this model like a real volcano?

2. How is this model different from a real volcano?

Inquire Further

How could you make your volcano erupt with more force?

What resources do we get from the earth?

You have probably seen sprinklers used for watering lawns. The sprinklers in this picture are used for watering large fields.

Water is used in many ways. You can use water for drinking, cooking, and washing. Water is a natural resource. **Natural resources** are useful materials that come from the earth.

Oil, coal, and gas are also natural resources. They are used for fuel. Fuel heats homes and other buildings. It helps run factories and machines. Oil is also made into gasoline for cars and trucks.

Forests are another natural resource. Trees are cut into lumber to build homes. Wood also can be burned for fuel.

How are natural resources being used in the pictures?

Lesson Review

1. Name some natural resources.

2. What are some ways fuel is used?

3. **Draw** two ways you use water every day.

How can you help protect the earth?

Think about the last time you threw something away. What was it? Could you have used it again instead of throwing it away?

When trash piles up, the earth gets dirty. Dirty air, water, and land can be harmful to people and animals. You can help protect the earth by keeping it clean. Don't litter. Use things over and over instead of throwing them away.

You can help by recycling too. **Recycling** means making new things from old things. You can recycle cans, bottles, and newspapers.

You can even recycle your leftover food scraps! Use them to make compost, and add the compost to your soil to help your plants grow.

Make compost.

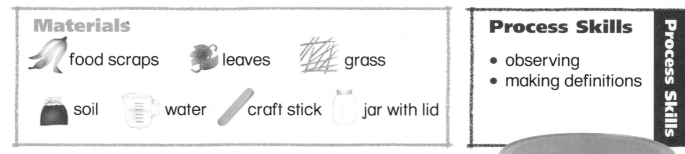

Materials

food scraps   leaves   grass

soil   water   craft stick   jar with lid

Process Skills

- observing
- making definitions

Process Skills

Steps

1 Put food scraps, leaves, grass, and soil into the jar.

2 Add a little water. Stir with the craft stick. Cover the jar.

3 **Observe** the jar every day.

4 **Make a definition.** Tell what compost means.

Share. Describe your compost.

Lesson Review

1. How can you help protect the earth?

2. What is recycling?

3. **Draw** your compost after five days.

What can be recycled?

This playground may look like an ordinary playground. It is actually made completely from reused and recycled objects!

Reused objects are things that are used again and again. How are tires being reused in this playground?

Many of the things you use every day can be recycled. Cans, bottles, and newspapers can all be recycled to create new products. What did you use today that can be recycled?

Lesson Review

1. What does reuse mean?

2. What is special about the playground in the picture?

3. **Write** a list of some things that can be reused or recycled.

Chapter 1 Review

Reviewing Science Words

1. How do plant roots help prevent **erosion**?
2. What is **lava**?
3. Name three **natural resources**.
4. How does **recycling** protect the earth?

Reviewing Science Ideas

1. Name three features of the earth.
2. What words can you use to describe rocks?
3. What happens during an earthquake?
4. What can you do to help protect the earth?

Tell about the earth.

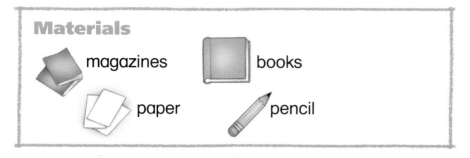

Materials

magazines   books

paper   pencil

① Find a picture that shows some features of the earth.

② Write some sentences that tell about your picture.

③ Display your picture with classmates' pictures.

④ Take turns reading your sentences aloud.

⑤ Match the sentences and pictures.

Chapter 2
Weather and Seasons

Then I'll Know

🎵 Sing to the tune of *Picking Up Pawpaws*.

Is the temperature high or low?

Up or down, which way will it go?

I'll check a thermometer and then I'll know.

The temperature is part of the weather.

Is the wind blowing fast or slow?

And what direction does it blow?

I'll check the windsock and then I'll know.

The wind is part of the weather.

Up in the sky I see a rainbow,

It must have rained, not long ago.

I'll check the rain gauge and then I'll know.

The rain is part of the weather.

Original lyrics by Gerri Brioso and Richard Freitas.
Produced by Children's Television Workshop.

What can you tell about the weather?

Look outside. What is the weather like today? It may be hot or cold, or sunny or cloudy. Does the picture below show a windy or calm day?

You can tell a lot about the weather just by looking outside. Scientists use tools to measure things about the weather. A **thermometer** measures the temperature of the air. An **anemometer** like the one at the right measures how fast the wind is blowing.

Make an anemometer.

Materials

safety goggles   l straw

push pin   2 small cups

unsharpened pencil with eraser

Process Skills

- estimating and measuring

Steps

1 Put on your safety goggles.

2 Make an anemometer like the one in the picture.

3 Use your anemometer to **measure** the wind.

4 Go to different places.

Share. Tell how you can make your anemometer go around faster or slower.

Lesson Review

1. How can scientists measure the temperature of the air?

2. How can scientists measure how fast the wind is blowing?

3. **Show** how an anemometer can measure the wind.

Using Measurement Tools

You can use a thermometer to measure temperature. When the red line goes up, that means it is getting warmer. When the red line goes down, it is getting colder.

The number next to the top of the red line is the temperature. These numbers are called degrees.

When you write the temperature, you can use a small circle to stand for degrees.

This thermometer shows that it is 30° Celsius.

How many degrees does this thermometer show?

Turn the page to do an activity using a thermometer.

Turn the page.

Experiment with temperature.

Process Skills

- experimenting
- estimating and measuring

Materials

3 cups   3 thermometers

soil   water   clock

Problem

How do the temperatures of soil, water, and air change after being placed in the sunlight?

Give Your Hypothesis

If you put soil, water, and air in sunlight, will their temperatures go up or down? Tell what you think.

Control the Variables

Make sure that each cup is placed in the same amount of sunlight for the same amount of time.

Test Your Hypothesis

Follow these steps to do the **experiment**.

1. Fill one cup with soil, one with water, and leave one for air.

2. **Measure** the temperature inside each cup.

3 Put all three cups in direct sunlight.

4 **Measure** the temperature inside each cup after 30 minutes.

Collect Your Data

Use a chart like this one. Record the starting temperatures and the temperatures after 30 minutes.

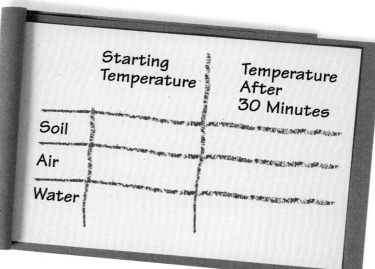

	Starting Temperature	Temperature After 30 Minutes
Soil		
Air		
Water		

Tell Your Conclusion

Compare your results and hypothesis. How do the temperatures of soil, water, and air change after being placed in the sunlight?

Inquire Further

What would happen to the temperatures if you put the cups in a shady place?

soil   air   water

What happens in spring and summer?

The four seasons are spring, summer, fall, and winter. Which season do you like best?

In the spring, the air may be cool or warm. In many places, spring is the rainiest season of the year. Buds and leaves begin to grow on plants. Birds and other animals have babies. What signs of spring do you see in these pictures?

Spring in New Jersey

Summer in Florida

In many places, summer is the hottest season of the year. Trees and other plants have lots of green leaves. Flowers bloom and many fruits and vegetables grow. It is summer in these pictures.

What are spring and summer like where you live?

Lesson Review

1. What happens in spring?

2. What happens in summer?

3. **Draw** a picture of how your neighborhood looks in spring or summer.

What happens in fall and winter?

Are days and nights chilly? Do crisp leaves crunch under your feet? What are some signs of fall near your home?

In many places, fall starts out warm and grows cooler. Many plants stop growing. Leaves change colors and drop from the trees. Many animals store food to prepare for the coming winter. What are some signs of fall in these pictures?

Fall in Michigan

Winter in Illinois

In many places, winter brings
cold air and snow. Water in ponds
or lakes can freeze. Many trees have
no leaves at all. Some animals hibernate,
or sleep, all winter long. How can you tell it is
winter in these pictures?

What are fall and winter like where you live?

Lesson Review

1. What do many animals do in the fall?

2. What is the weather like in the winter?

3. **Tell** how fall and winter are different.

Is there water in air?

Drip, drop, drip, drop. Rain is falling. Puddles form on the ground. What happens to a puddle after the rain stops?

Over time, the water in the puddle evaporates. When water **evaporates** it changes into a gas called water vapor.

The water vapor rises into the air. It cools and condenses into tiny drops of water. When water vapor **condenses** , it changes from a gas to a liquid. The tiny drops of water form clouds. Some of the drops freeze. If the air is cold, the drops fall as snow. If the air is warm, they fall as rain.

The way water moves from the clouds to the earth and back to the clouds again is called the **water cycle** . The picture shows the water cycle.

Clouds form.

Water vapor cools and condenses.

Rain forms.

Water evaporates.

Observe the water cycle.

Materials

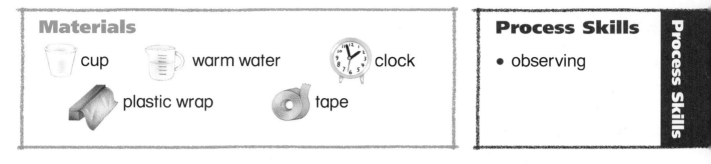

cup   warm water   clock

plastic wrap   tape

Process Skills

● observing

Process Skills

Steps

1. Fill your cup halfway with warm water.

2. Tape the plastic wrap over the top of the cup.

3. Put the cup in a sunny place for 30 minutes.

4. **Observe.**

Share. Tell how your cup shows the water cycle.

Lesson Review

1. What does evaporate mean?

2. What is the water cycle?

3. **Draw** how your cup and plastic wrap look after 30 minutes.

How does water vapor condense?

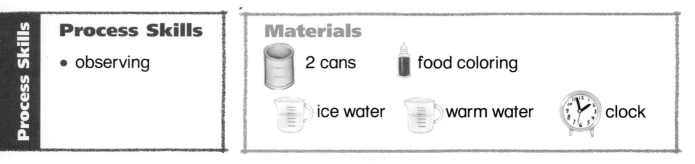

Process Skills

- observing

Materials

2 cans   food coloring

ice water   warm water   clock

Steps

1. Fill one can halfway with warm water.

2. Fill one can halfway with ice water.

3. Add two or three drops of food coloring to each can.

4. Wait five minutes.

5. Look at the cans. What changes do you see on the outside of each can?

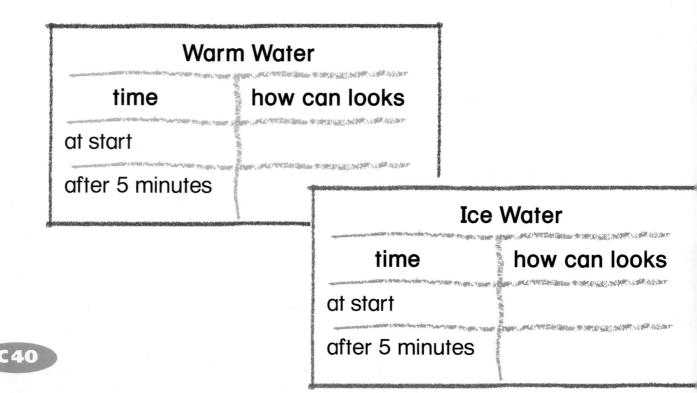

Warm Water

time	how can looks
at start	
after 5 minutes	

Ice Water

time	how can looks
at start	
after 5 minutes	

Think About Your Results

1. How do the cans look different?

2. What caused the water vapor to condense?

? Inquire Further

What are some other places that show water that condensed from water vapor in the air?

What are some kinds of bad weather?

Flash! Boom! You see lightning and hear thunder! A storm is coming.

A thunderstorm is a heavy rain with lightning and thunder. Never stand under a tree during a thunderstorm. Go indoors as soon as you can. If you are swimming, get out of the water quickly.

A **tornado** is a very strong wind storm. If there is a tornado warning, stay indoors and away from windows. Go to the basement or the lowest part of the building that you are in.

Lightning Storm
Stay indoors or
low to the ground.

If a lot of rain falls in a short time, there can be a flood. Flood water is not safe to play in. To stay safe, go to a place that is higher than the water.

If it has not rained in a long time, a **drought** can occur. During a drought, the land is very dry and there is very little water available.

What other kinds of bad weather do you know about?

Lesson Review

1. How can you stay safe in a thunderstorm?

2. If you hear a warning about a tornado, what should you do?

3. **Tell** how a flood and a drought are different.

Tornado
Stay indoors away from windows.

Flood
Stay on high ground.

STOP

Chapter 2 Review

Reviewing Science Words

1. What does a **thermometer** measure?

2. What does an **anemometer** measure?

3. Describe what happens when water **evaporates**.

4. What happens when water vapor **condenses**?

5. Describe the **water cycle**.

6. What is a **tornado**?

7. When can a **drought** occur?

Reviewing Science Ideas

1. How can scientists measure the weather?

2. Name some signs of spring, summer, fall, and winter.

3. Name some ways to stay safe in bad weather.

Draw one place in two seasons.

Materials

 paper

markers or crayons

1. Choose two seasons of the year.

2. Think about how these two seasons are different.

3. Draw a place, such as a park or a pond, in one season of the year.

4. Then draw the same place in the other season you have chosen.

5. Compare your drawings. How do they look different? How do they look the same?

The Solar System

Up in the Sky

♫ Sing to the tune of *The Eensy Weensy Spider*.

The planets and their moons and the sun up in the sky

Make up our solar system stretching far and wide.

The Earth and other planets all spin around the sun.

What spins around the Earth and can be seen by everyone?

Round and round the Earth spins a moon that's all our own.

With mountains and craters that are hard as stone.

The moon seems to change from full to very thin.

Did you notice it last night? Did it look just like a grin?

A telescope is handy to look up in the sky.

As you're looking through it, the stars will catch your eye.

You may see some stars that are dim and far away.

Can you name the star that's brightest and shines on us each day?

Original lyrics by Gerri Brioso and Richard Freitas.
Produced by Children's Television Workshop.

C47

What causes day and night?

Stand up and spin around! How do you feel? You may be dizzy.

Did you know Earth is spinning too? Even though you cannot feel it, Earth is always turning.

Day and night happen because Earth turns. When your side of Earth is facing the sun, you have daytime. When your side of Earth is not facing the sun, you have nighttime.

We say that the sun rises and sets, but really the sun does not. The sun only seems to move across the sky. It looks like it is moving because Earth is moving.

Look at the picture. Find the part of Earth that is facing the sun. It is daytime there. Which part of Earth would have nighttime?

Sun

Earth

Show how Earth rotates.

Materials

 globe   stickers   flashlight

Process Skills

- observing

Process Skills

Steps

1 Put the globe on a desk or table.

2 Put your sticker where you live.

3 Shine the flashlight on the globe.

4 Spin the globe. Let it stop on its own.

5 **Observe** whether your sticker ends up in daytime or nighttime.

Share. Show a friend which side of the globe is in daytime and which is in nighttime.

Lesson Review

1. Why do day and night happen?

2. When do you have nighttime?

3. **Draw** a picture of Earth and the sun. Label the day and night sides of Earth.

What do we know about the moon?

Think about what you see in the sky at night. You have probably seen the moon. Have you ever wondered what the moon is like?

The moon is not like Earth. The moon has rocks and soil, but it does not have air or living things. Ice has been found on the moon.

Look at the picture of the surface of the moon. You can see craters. A **crater** is a hole in the ground that is shaped like a bowl. These craters were made long ago when rocks from space crashed into the moon.

What does the moon look like to you? It may look like it has a different shape every day.

The moon seems to change shape because you only see the part that has light shining on it. The rest of the moon looks dark to you.

The shapes that you see are called the **phases** of the moon. These pictures show some of the moon's phases. It takes about a month to see all the phases of the moon.

Lesson Review

1. What are craters?

2. Why does the moon seem to change shape?

3. **Draw** two phases of the moon.

How can you record the phases of the moon?

Process Skills

- collecting and interpreting data
- observing

Materials

 calendar

 crayons or markers

Steps

1. Start with a blank calendar.

2. Fill in all the dates for this month.

3. **Collect data** by **observing** the moon every night for one month.

4. On your calendar, draw how the moon looks every night.

Think About Your Results

1. In what ways did the moon look different every night?

2. Do any of your pictures look the same? If so, which ones?

Inquire Further

Would your data be the same or different next month? How could you find out?

October

Tuesday	Wednesday	Thursday	Friday	Saturday
1	2	3	4	5
		10	11	12
7		17	18	19
14		24	25	26
21	22			
30				

Using Picture Clues

You can use pictures to get information. Use the picture to answer these questions.

Astronauts have landed on the moon. What did the astronauts do when they got there? What did they bring with them? What else can you learn from looking at the picture?

Look at the picture on this page. Write one thing about the picture. Ask a friend to write one thing about the picture.

Share what you wrote. Did you both write the same thing?

How many other things can you write about the picture? Share your ideas.

Turn the page to find out how pictures can help you learn about the solar system.

Turn the page.

What is in our solar system?

Did you know that there is a star you can see during the day? Which star is it? It is the sun!

The sun is in the center of our solar system. All of the planets in our solar system orbit the sun. To **orbit** means to move around another object along a path. What else can you learn about the solar system from this picture?

Saturn

Neptune

Uranus

Pluto

Jupiter

Venus

Mercury

Earth

Sun

Mars

Lesson Review

1. What is in the center of our solar system?

2. What does orbit mean?

3. **Tell** what is in our solar system.

How do we learn about the solar system?

What do you see when you look at the sky? You may see the sun, moon, or stars. How could you get a better look at the sky?

Scientists use telescopes to look at parts of the solar system. A **telescope** makes objects that are far away look closer.

Scientists have other ways of learning about the solar system too. They can send cameras and other equipment into space to take pictures and collect information. They can also send astronauts into space.

What would you like to know about the solar system?

▲ A satellite that collects information in space

◀ Telescope

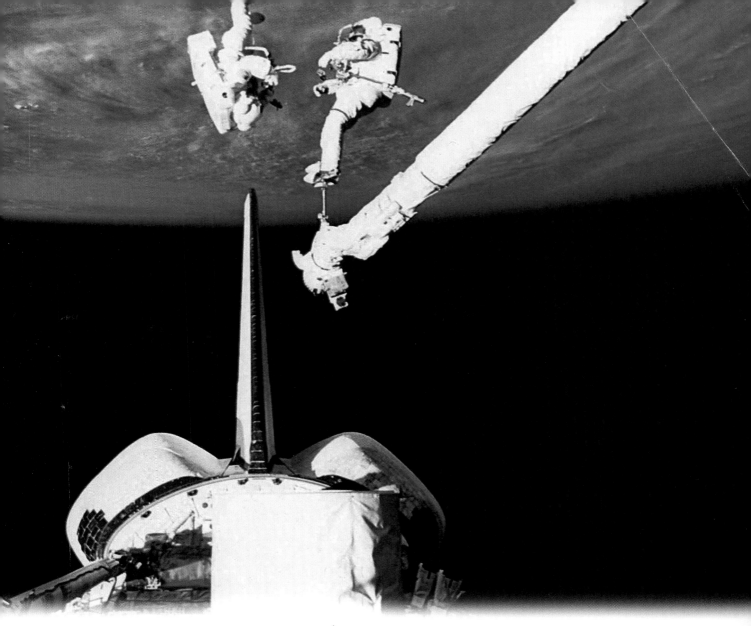

▲ Astronauts in space

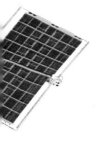

Lesson Review

1. What does a telescope do?

2. What are some reasons scientists send astronauts into space?

3. **Tell** some ways scientists learn about the solar system.

Chapter 3 Review

Reviewing Science Words

1. What are **phases** of the moon?

2. How did **craters** form on the moon?

3. What **orbits** the sun?

4. How does a **telescope** help scientists learn about the solar system?

Reviewing Science Ideas

1. What causes day and night?

2. Why does the moon seem to change shape?

3. What is in our solar system?

4. How do scientists learn about the solar system?

Show the phases of the moon.

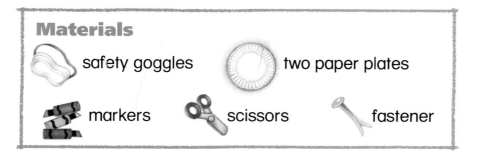

Materials

safety goggles   two paper plates   markers   scissors   fastener

1. Put on your safety goggles.

2. On one plate, draw some phases of the moon in order around the outer edge.

3. On the other plate, draw where you live. Cut a hole above your picture.

4. Put the plate with the hole on top of the other plate.

5. Use your scissors to make a small hole in the center of both plates. Hold them together with the fastener.

6. To see the phases of the moon, turn the bottom plate.

Unit C
Performance Review

If you could go anywhere on the earth, where would you go? What if you could visit the sun, moon, and stars too? Think about an adventure you would like to have. Where could you go? What would you see?

Plan your adventure.

1. Pick a project to show something you have learned.

2. What steps will you follow to complete your project?

3. How will your project look when you finish it?

Make a backpack.

What will you take on your adventure? What clothes or gear will you need? Will you bring food? Make a backpack for your adventure. Make things to put inside. Show your classmates what is in your backpack. Tell how you will use these things.

Talk to a friend.

Pretend that you just got back from your adventure. Telephone a friend to describe the places you visited. Tell about land, water, and other things you saw. What else will you tell your friend about your adventure? What questions might your friend ask you?

Write a postcard.

Think of a place you visited on your adventure. What did you see? What was the weather like? What did you do? Write a postcard. Draw a picture on your postcard to go with your message.

Writing an Ad

When you persuade people, you get them to do something. You can also persuade people that something is important. Write an ad to persuade people. Draw pictures and write sentences for your ad.

1. **Prewrite** Think of reasons to recycle. How can you persuade people to recycle?

2. **Draft** Write an ad that will persuade people to recycle.

3. **Revise** Read your ad. Will it persuade people to recycle?

4. **Edit** Check your writing to make sure it is correct. Make a neat copy.

5. **Publish** Share your ad with others. Did you persuade them to recycle?

Unit D
Human Body

Science and Technology
In Your World!

How can scientists see the brain at work?

A special machine takes pictures of the brain. The pictures show what happens in the brain as a person thinks, learns, and remembers.

Chapter 1
The Human Body

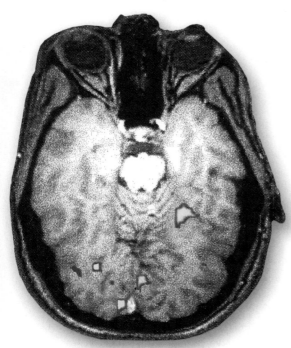

Scientists can make flour from fruits.

They use the pulp and rind. This flour has vitamins, minerals, and fiber that are important for a person's diet.

Chapter 2
Nutrition

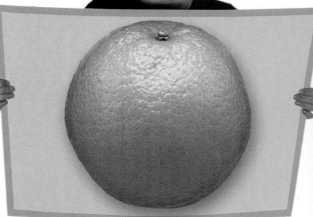

A special exhibit is visiting science museums.

The exhibit has pictures made with light, models that move, and unusual kinds of toys. The exhibit helps people learn about germs.

Chapter 3
Keeping Healthy

How Your Body Works

Sing to the tune of *Polly Wolly Doodle*.

Oh, your brain and nerves work together so hard.

They never stop, they're working all day.

Your nerves tell your brain what's going on.

And it makes decisions right away.

When you breathe your lungs go right to work.

Air comes in, then out it goes.

While your heart keeps working by pumping your blood

From your head down to your toes.

Never stops.

Always works.

It's amazing what your body can do.

Always working, always thinking,

Always breathing, always pumping,

All together, working hard for you!

Original lyrics by Gerri Brioso and Richard Freitas.
Produced by Children's Television Workshop.
Copyright ©1999 Sesame Street, Inc.

What does the brain do?

Imagine a ball coming your way. You run, reach out your arm, and try to catch it!

Your **brain** controls what your body does. You use your brain to move, think, feel, and remember.

Your brain sends and receives messages through your nerves. **Nerves** are the pathways that lead to and from your brain. They go through your whole body.

When you see, hear, feel, taste, or touch something, this information travels through your nerves to your brain. Your brain sends messages to the other parts of your body.

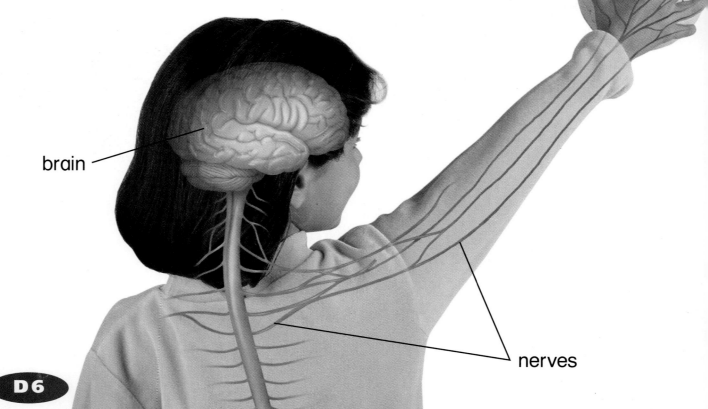

brain

nerves

Play a catching game.

Materials

ruler

Process Skills

- collecting and interpreting data

Steps

1. Work with a partner. Take turns.

2. Have your partner hold the ruler above your fingers and then drop it.

3. Try to catch the ruler between your thumb and index finger.

4. Do this activity five times. How many times were you able to catch the ruler? **Collect** and record your data.

Share. Tell what happened.

Lesson Review

1. What does the brain do?

2. What are nerves?

3. **Tell** what your brain has to do to help you catch the ruler.

Reading Labels

Some pictures and diagrams have labels. Labels give you information about the picture or diagram.

Labels can be next to a picture or underneath it. Sometimes a label has a line going from the label to the part of the picture it tells about.

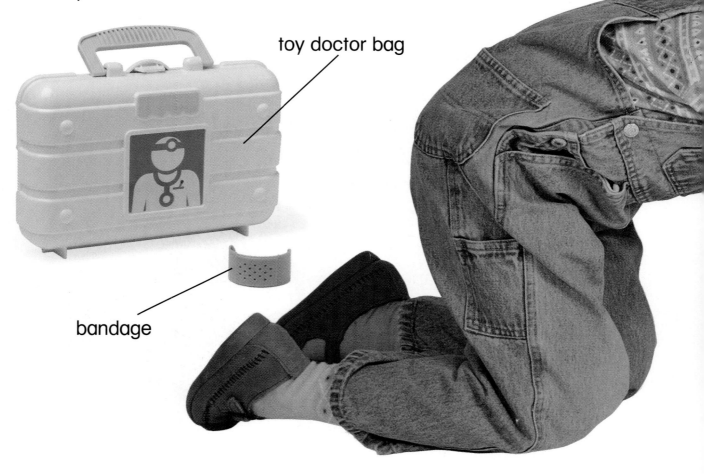

toy doctor bag

bandage

This picture shows a girl playing. How do the labels help you understand what she is pretending to be?

dog

stethoscope

Turn the page to find out how labels can help you learn more about the human body.

Turn the page.

What do the heart and lungs do?

Take a deep breath. Let it out. Your body does a lot of work with just one breath!

When you breathe, your **lungs** take in air. Air contains oxygen, a gas that your whole body needs. Oxygen enters your lungs first. The oxygen needs to reach the rest of your body too.

Your **heart** pumps blood to every part of your body. Blood contains materials that your body needs. When your heart pumps blood to your lungs, the blood picks up oxygen from the lungs. Then the blood carries the oxygen to all parts of your body.

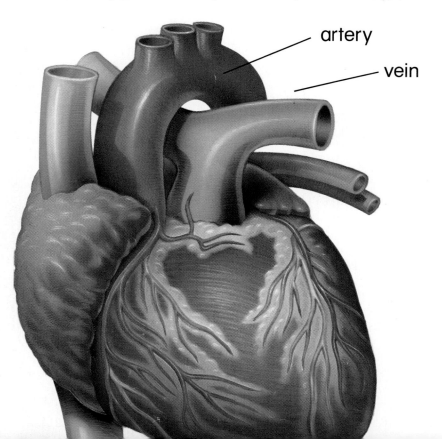

artery

vein

Blood is pumped away from your heart in tubes called **arteries**. Then it travels back to the heart in tubes called **veins**.

Your heart and lungs work together to keep you healthy.

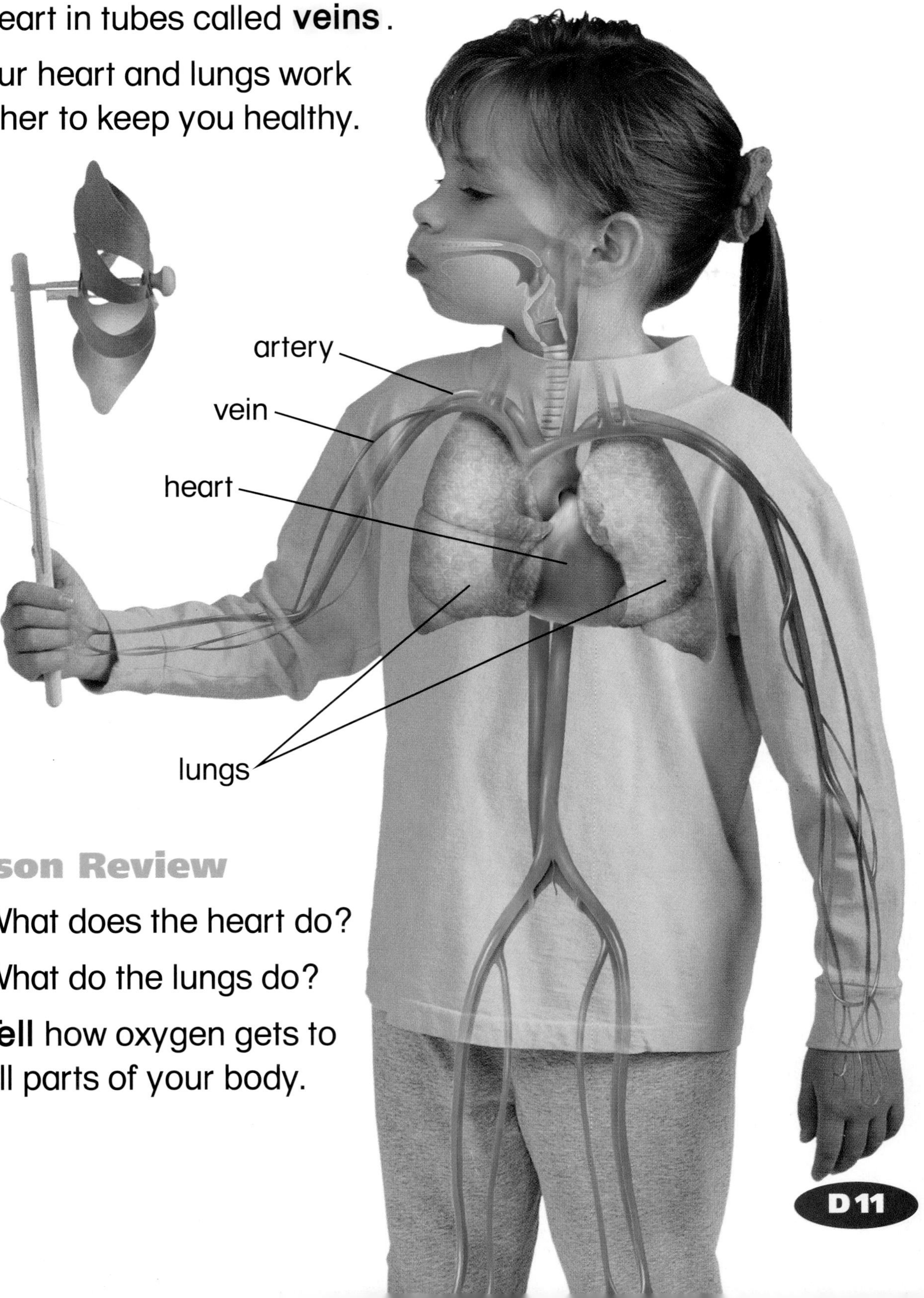

artery

vein

heart

lungs

Lesson Review

1. What does the heart do?

2. What do the lungs do?

3. **Tell** how oxygen gets to all parts of your body.

How long can you blow bubbles?

Process Skills

- predicting
- collecting and interpreting data

Materials

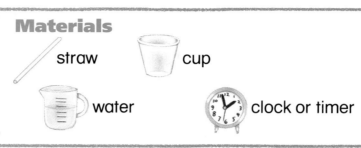

straw   cup

water   clock or timer

Steps

1. Fill a cup halfway with water.

2. How long can you blow bubbles without stopping? **Predict.**

3. Put your straw into your cup. Do not let the straw touch the bottom of the cup.

4. Blow bubbles for as long as you can. Have your partner time you.

5. How long did you blow bubbles? **Collect** and record your data.

6. Trade places with your partner. Do the activity again.

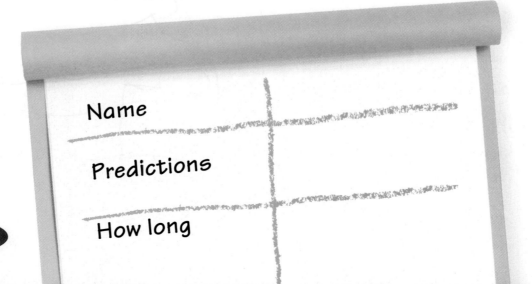

Name

Predictions

How long

Think About Your Results

1. How long were you able to blow bubbles?

2. How close was your prediction to your results?

🔍 Inquire Further

How could you blow bubbles for a longer amount
of time?

Experiment with exercise.

Process Skills

- experimenting
- estimating and measuring

Materials

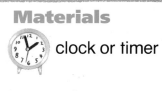 clock or timer

Problem

How does exercise affect your heart rate?

Give Your Hypothesis

How will your heart rate change when you exercise? Tell what you think.

Control the Variables

Make sure you measure your heart rate for the same amount of time before and after running.

Test Your Hypothesis

Follow these steps to do the **experiment**.

1. Sit quietly. **Measure** your heart rate by taking your pulse for 30 seconds. Have your partner keep track of the time.

2. Now run in place for one minute. Have your partner keep track of the time.

③ Measure your heart rate for 30 seconds again. Have your partner keep track of the time.

④ Trade places with your partner. Do the activity again.

Collect Your Data

Use a chart like this one. Record your heart rate while sitting and after running.

Activity	Heart Rate for 30 Seconds
sitting	_____
after running	_____

Tell Your Conclusion

Compare your results and hypothesis. How does exercise affect your heart rate?

Inquire Further

If you exercised for more than one minute, how would this affect your heart rate?

Chapter 1 Review

Reviewing Science Words

1. Name two things the **brain** does.

2. What do the **nerves** do?

3. What do the **lungs** take into the body?

4. What does the **heart** do?

5. What are **arteries** ?

6. What are **veins** ?

Reviewing Science Ideas

1. How do the heart and lungs work together?

2. How does exercise affect your heart rate?

Draw a diagram of your body.

Materials

 paper    crayons

1 Draw an outline of your body.

2 Draw your brain, lungs, and heart in the correct places. Label them.

3 You can use the pictures in this chapter to help you.

4 Tell a friend about your drawing.

Chapter 2
Nutrition

Good to Eat

♫ Sing to the tune of *Alouette*.

There are foods that help us all stay healthy.

And there are foods that give us energy.

Let's name some foods we like to eat.

Like fruit and cheese and milk and meat.

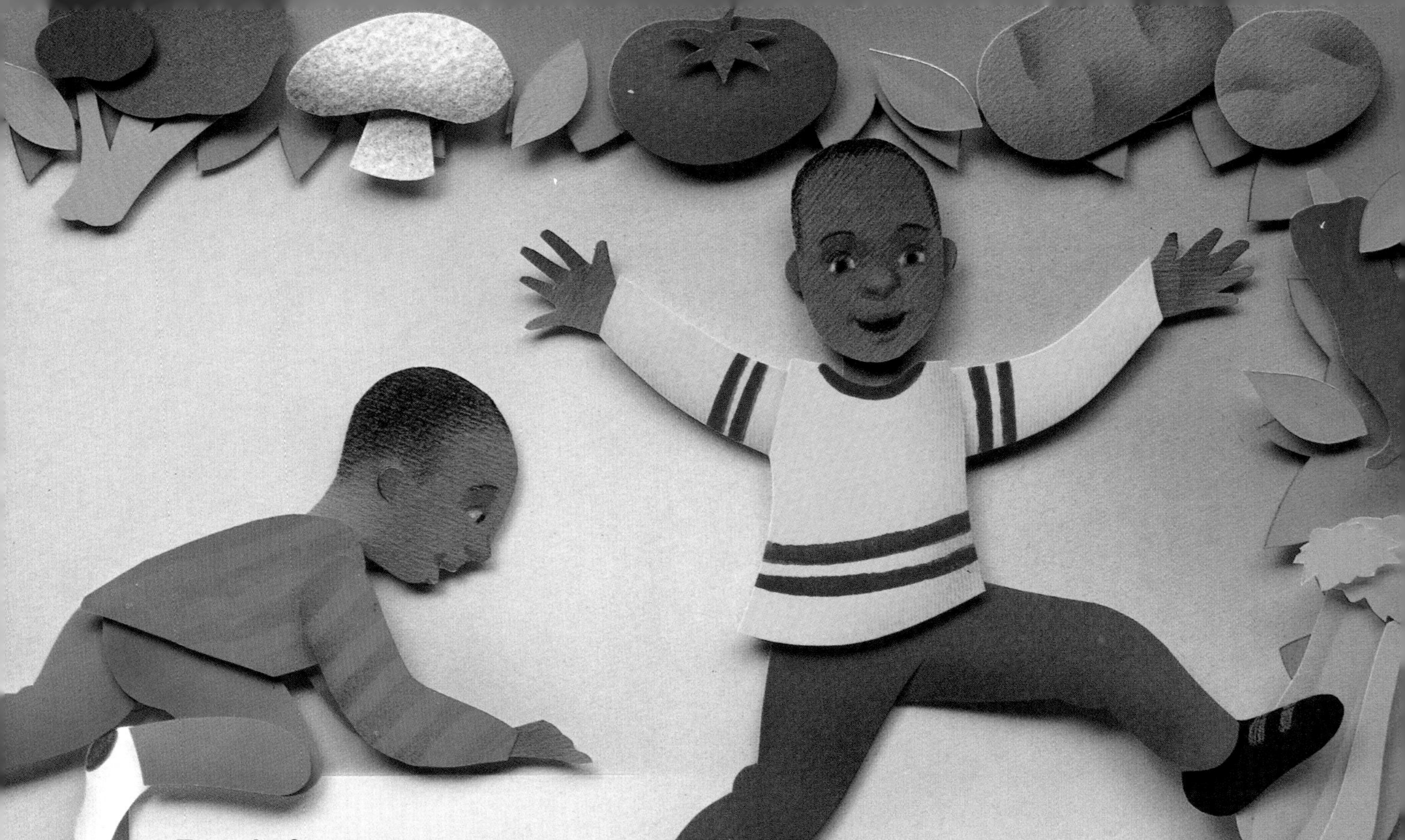

Don't forget,
Bread and rice.
Vegetables,
Are very nice.
Fish and beans,
With some spice.
Cereal,
Have it twice.
Oh, oh, oh, oh,
There are foods that help us all stay healthy.
And when we're healthy, we grow and grow and grow.

Original lyrics by Gerri Brioso and Richard Freitas.
Produced by Children's Television Workshop.

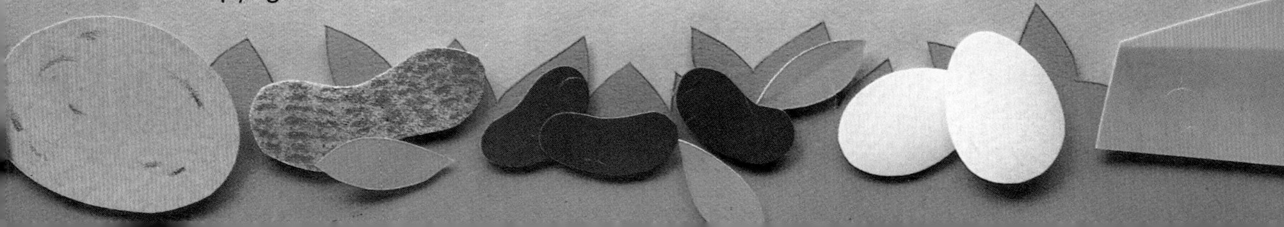

Using a Diagram

A diagram gives information in a chart or picture instead of sentences.

The diagram on page D21 tells what this child likes to do in her free time. The bottom section is the biggest. This tells you that she spends most of her free time riding her bike.

She spends the least amount of her free time coloring. You can tell because that section is the smallest.

Does she spend more time watching TV or reading? How do you know?

How Ann Spends Her Free Time

Color

Watch TV

Read Books

Ride My Bike

Turn the page to find out how a diagram can help you learn about food.

Turn the page.

What foods help you stay healthy?

What is your favorite food? You may like that food because it tastes good. Did you know that food helps keep you healthy?

Food gives you energy to work and play. It also helps you grow. To stay healthy, you need to eat certain kinds of foods every day.

The **Food Guide Pyramid** shows the food groups. It also shows how many servings you should eat every day from each food group. To stay healthy, eat more foods from the bottom of the pyramid and fewer foods from the top.

The Food Guide Pyramid

Fats, Oils, and Sweets
Use sparingly.

Milk, Yogurt, and Cheese Group
2–3 Servings

Meat, Poultry, Fish, Dry Beans, Eggs, and Nuts Group
2–3 Servings

Vegetable Group
3–5 Servings

Fruit Group
2–4 Servings

Bread, Cereal, Rice, and Pasta
6–11 Servings

Make a Food Guide Pyramid.

Materials

large piece of paper scissors

glue magazines or newspapers

Process Skills

- classifying

Steps

1. Draw a Food Guide Pyramid. Label each section.

2. Cut out pictures of food from magazines or newspapers.

3. **Classify** each picture into one of the food groups.

4. Glue the pictures onto the Food Guide Pyramid.

Share. Explain your Food Guide Pyramid to a friend.

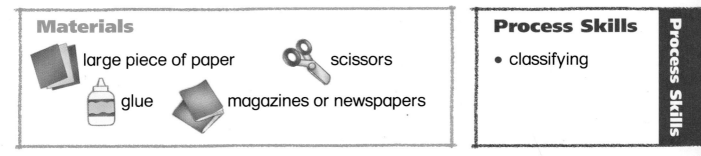

Lesson Review

1. Why is food important?

2. What does the Food Guide Pyramid show?

3. **Tell** what food group your favorite food is in.

Which foods will leave a greasy spot?

Process Skills

- predicting
- collecting and interpreting data

Materials

clean brown paper bag   marker

butter   carrot   snack foods

Steps

1. Draw four large circles on your bag.

2. Label one circle Butter. Label another circle Carrot. Label the last two circles with the snack foods you will test.

3. Use a chart like this one.

Food   Prediction   Results

4. If you rub each food on your bag, which ones will leave a greasy spot? **Predict.**

5. **Collect data** by rubbing each food on your bag.

6. Hold your bag up to the light. Which foods left a greasy spot?

7. Record your results.

Think About Your Results

1. Which foods left a greasy spot?

2. Which foods did not leave a greasy spot?

Inquire Further

What other foods do you think would leave a greasy spot?

Carrot

Butter

What happens when you chew?

Think about biting into a crisp apple. It might taste cool and sweet. It might feel crunchy in your mouth.

You know that food gives your body energy. Food needs to be broken down and changed so your body can use it. The process of breaking down food is called **digestion**.

Digestion begins in your mouth. When you chew, your teeth grind the food into small pieces. Your saliva makes the food wet, and your tongue mixes it. The food has started to change.

Observe how food can be changed.

Materials

2 resealable plastic bags

2 soda crackers   water

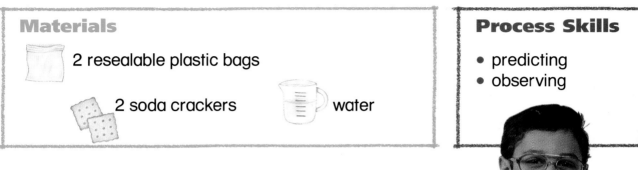

Process Skills

- predicting
- observing

Process Skills

Steps

1. Put one cracker in each bag.

2. Break one of the crackers into small pieces. Leave the other cracker whole.

3. Add water to both bags. Seal the bags.

4. What will happen to the crackers if you shake the bags? **Predict.**

5. Shake each bag ten times. **Observe.**

Share. Compare the crackers.

Lesson Review

1. What is digestion?

2. What happens to food when you chew it?

3. **Tell** how chewing and saliva help digestion.

How is food digested?

What did you have for dinner last night? After you chewed and swallowed your food, where did it go?

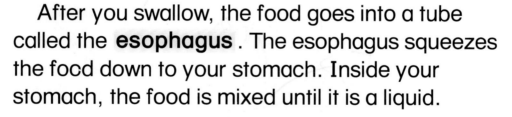

After you swallow, the food goes into a tube called the **esophagus** . The esophagus squeezes the food down to your stomach. Inside your stomach, the food is mixed until it is a liquid.

Next, the liquid goes into the small intestine. The **small intestine** is a long, thin tube that is curled up. Most of the digestion takes place in the small intestine. You need nutrients from the digested food. **Nutrients** are materials in food that you need to grow and stay healthy.

The leftover liquid goes into the large intestine. The **large intestine** squeezes out the rest of the liquid and then passes solid wastes out of the body.

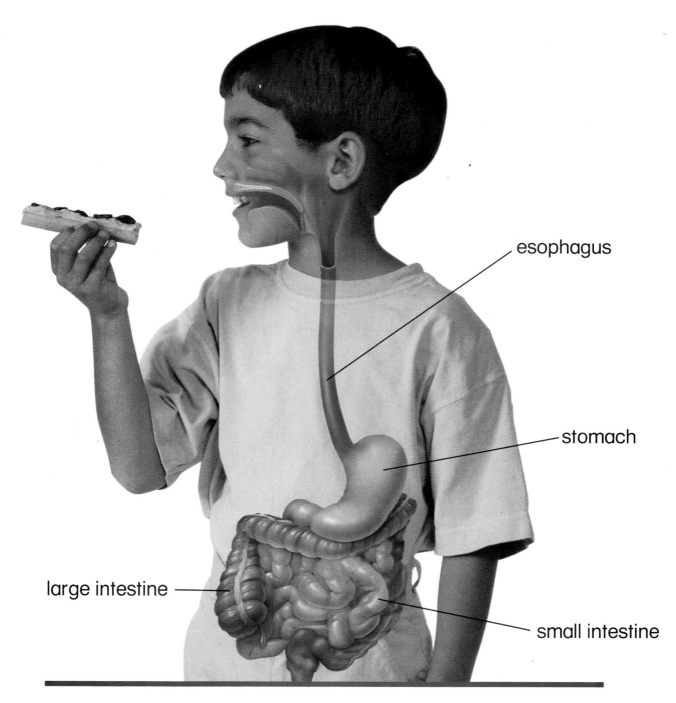

esophagus

stomach

large intestine

small intestine

Lesson Review

1. What happens inside the stomach?

2. Where does most of the digestion take place?

3. **Draw** the path food takes through the body.

Chapter 2 Review

Reviewing Science Words

1. How does the **Food Guide Pyramid** help you stay healthy?

2. Where does **digestion** begin?

3. What does the **esophagus** do?

4. What happens in the **small intestine**?

5. How do **nutrients** help you?

6. What does the **large intestine** do?

Reviewing Science Ideas

1. Name three of the food groups.

2. Explain how food is digested.

Make a daily menu.

Materials

paper

pencil or markers

1. Work with a group.

2. Talk about what you like to eat for breakfast, lunch, and dinner.

3. Use the Food Guide Pyramid to plan meals that have all the servings you need from each food group.

4. Make your menu and share it with the class.

Chapter 3
Keeping Healthy

Exercise Today

🎵 Sing to the tune of *Row, Row, Row, Your Boat*.

Exercise each day,

It's the thing to do.

Running, or jumping, or climbing a hill,

Whatever's fun for you.

Exercise will keep

Your muscles really strong.

So play some ball or take a walk.

With that, you can't go wrong.

Keep your lungs and heart
Healthy, don't delay.
Swim in a pool or ride a bike.
Exercise today!

Why is exercise important?

At recess, you may play a game, throw a ball, or take a walk. What do you like to do at recess?

When you are active, your body is getting exercise. You can get **exercise** by walking, running, swimming, playing, and doing many other activities. What kinds of exercise do you get every day?

Exercise helps your body stay healthy. It keeps your muscles strong and your heart and lungs healthy. How is the girl in the picture keeping herself healthy?

Do exercises.

Materials

 clock or stopwatch

Process Skills

- predicting
- collecting and interpreting data

Process Skills

Steps

1 How many jumping jacks can you do in one minute? **Predict.**

2 Take turns with your partner.

3 Do jumping jacks for one minute. Be sure to count each one.

4 Have your partner time you.

5 How many jumping jacks did you do? **Collect** and record your data.

Share. Compare your prediction with your results.

Lesson Review

1. Why is exercise important?

2. How can you get exercise?

3. **Show** a friend some exercises you can do in one minute.

Using a Calendar

A calendar tells you the name of the month, the days of the week, and the dates.

There are seven days in a week. The days of the week are always in order on a calendar. What is the first day of the week? What is the last day of the week?

The dates are always in order too. Sometimes the first day of the month is a Sunday and sometimes it is not.

Find March 8 on the calendar on page D37. What day of the week is it on?

Find the second Tuesday of the month. What is the date?

How many days are there in March?

March

Sunday	Monday	Tuesday	Wednesday	Thursday	Friday	Saturday
			1	2	3	4
5	6	7	8	9	10	11
12	13	14	15	16	17	18
19	20	21	22	23	24	25
26	27	28	29	30	31	

Turn the page to learn how a calendar can help you keep track of exercise.

Turn the page.

How much exercise do you get?

Process Skills

- collecting and interpreting data

Materials

 calendar   pencil or crayons

Steps

1. Label the month, days, and dates on your calendar.

2. **Collect data.** Draw or write how you got exercise each day.

Think About Your Results

1. What are some ways you got exercise?

2. How many different activities are on your calendar?

 Inquire Further

If you kept track of your daily exercise during a different month, would your activities be the same or different? Why?

Why is it important to keep clean?

It's bath time! You will need soap and water. Why do you need to take a bath?

A bath gets your body clean. You need to be clean to stay healthy.

Germs are tiny living things. Some germs can make you sick. Germs can be in the air and on things you touch.

Some germs can get into your body through your nose, mouth, or cuts in your skin. Washing with soap and water removes dirt and many germs.

It is important to wash your hands and scrub under your fingernails before you eat. This will help keep germs from getting into your body.

Brushing your teeth helps keep your mouth clean. If you brush every day, your teeth and gums will stay healthy.

What are some things you do to keep clean and stay healthy?

Lesson Review

1. What are germs?

2. Why is it important to brush your teeth?

3. **Tell** why it is important to keep your body clean.

How can you take care of yourself?

You eat healthful foods. You get exercise every day. You wash your hands and take a bath. These are good ways to take care of yourself.

Even though you take care of yourself, sometimes you still get hurt or sick.

If you get a cut or a scrape, show it to your parent or teacher. They can help you wash the area and cover it with a bandage.

Some days you might not feel well. You may have a fever. Your stomach may be upset. Let your parent or teacher know you do not feel well. You may need to stay home and rest until you feel better.

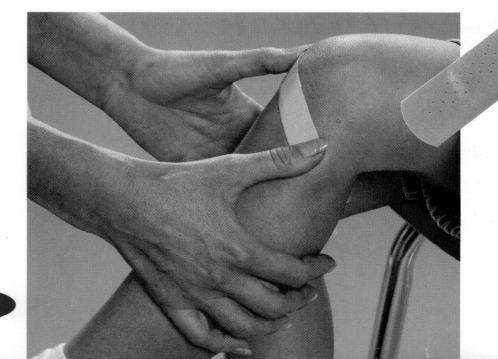

Sometimes you may need medicine to help your body fight an illness. Never take medicine by yourself. Only a trusted adult should give you medicine.

Visit your doctor for regular checkups. This will help you stay healthy.

Lesson Review

1. What can you do if you get a cut or a scrape?

2. What can you do if you do not feel well?

3. **Write** a list of some ways you can take care of yourself.

Chapter 3 Review

Reviewing Science Words

1. Name some ways you can get **exercise**.

2. How can **germs** get into your body?

Reviewing Science Ideas

1. How does exercise help your body?

2. What are some ways to keep your body clean?

3. Name some ways you can take care of yourself.

Put on a skit.

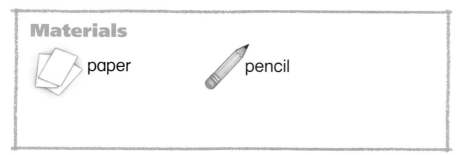

Materials

paper

pencil

1. Work with a group.

2. Make a list of ways to keep healthy.

3. Choose one thing to act out.

4. Plan a way to show your idea to the class.

5. Be sure each person in your group has a part.

6. Put on your skit for the class.

Unit D
Performance Review

How does your body work? What do you do to stay well? Have a health expo to show others what you know about health and the human body.

Plan your health expo.

1. Choose a project you would like to do.

2. Get materials you will need for your project.

3. Decide how you will show your project to your class.

Pack a lunch.

Plan a healthful lunch you would like. Draw a picture of each food or cut out pictures from magazines. Put the pictures in an empty lunch bag. Explain to others what you put in your lunch bag and why.

Play a guessing game.

Think of a part of the body you learned about in this unit. Have your partner ask questions that can be answered with a yes or no. Have your partner guess the part of the body.

Make a poster.

Make a poster about ways to get exercise. Draw pictures and write words on your poster. Remember to include a title.

Writing a Story

When you write a story, you tell about something that happened. If you write what happened in order, others will be able to understand your story.

1. **Prewrite** Think of things you did yesterday to stay healthy. Make a list to help plan your story. List things in the order that you did them.

2. **Draft** Write a story about yesterday. What healthful foods did you eat? How did you get exercise? Write your story in order. What happened first? Then what happened? What happened last?

3. **Revise** Read what you wrote. Do you want to change anything?

4. **Edit** Check your writing to make sure it is correct. Make a neat copy.

5. **Publish** Share your story with others. You can draw pictures too.

Your Science Handbook

⚠️ Safety in Science

Scientists do their experiments safely. You need to be careful when doing experiments too. The next page includes some safety tips to remember.

dish soap

- Read each experiment carefully.
- Wear safety goggles when needed.
- Clean up spills right away.
- Never taste or smell materials unless your teacher tells you to.
- Tape sharp edges of materials.
- Put things away when you finish an experiment.
- Wash your hands after each experiment.

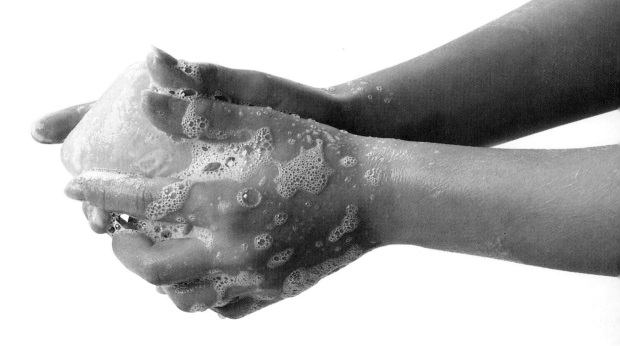

Using the Metric System

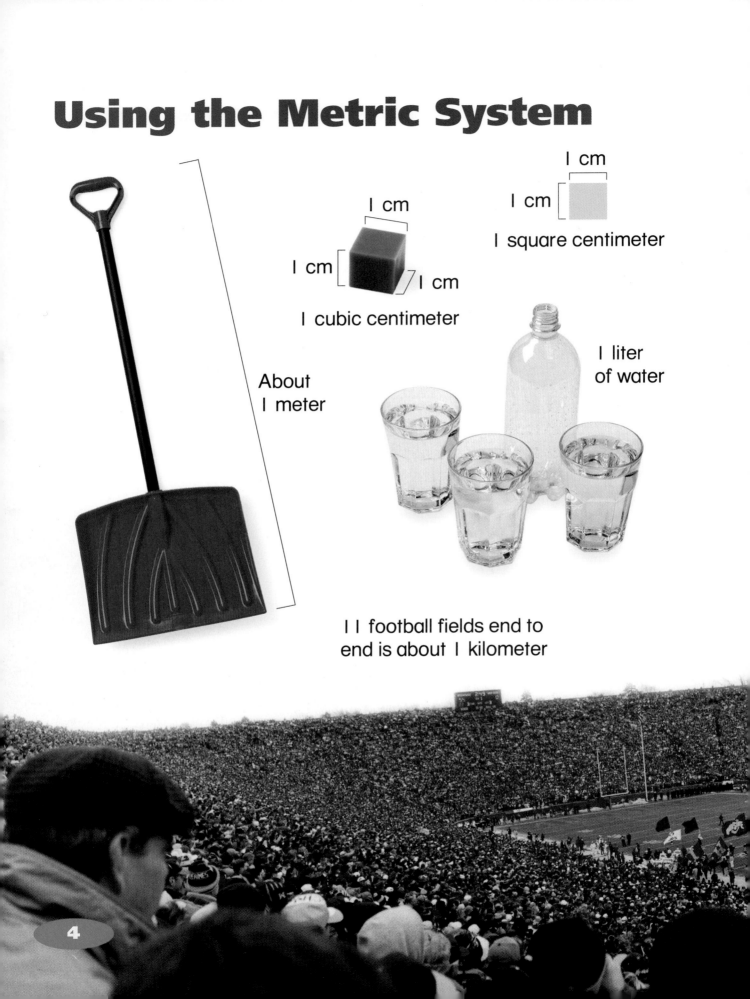

I cm

I cm
I cm
1 cubic centimeter

I cm
I cm
1 square centimeter

About
1 meter

1 liter
of water

11 football fields end to
end is about 1 kilometer

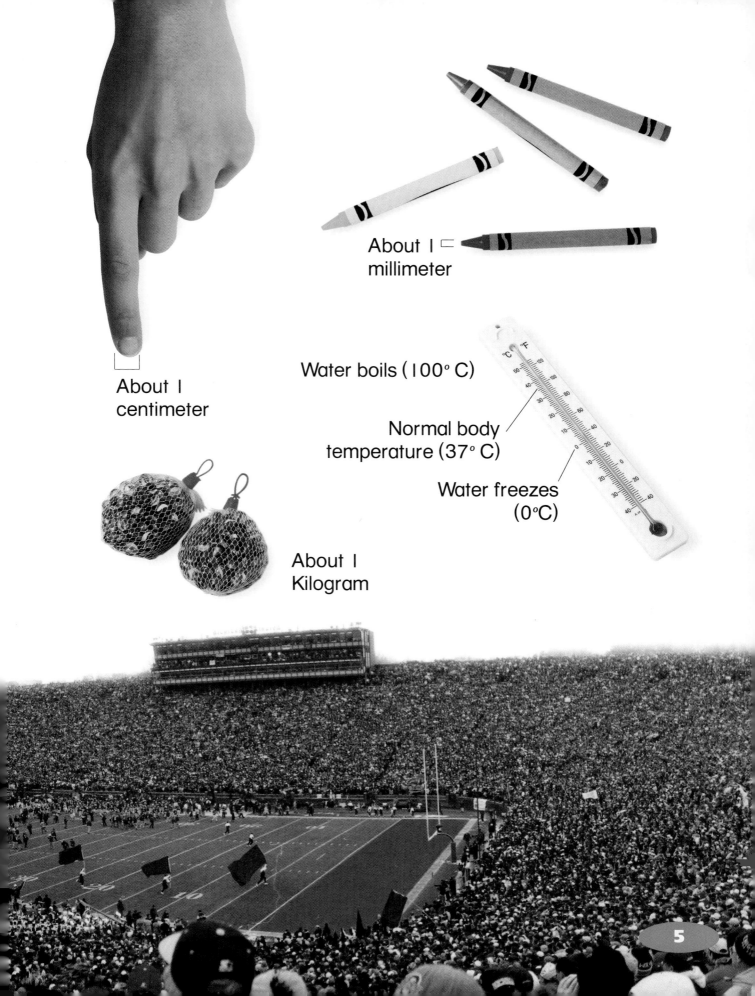

About 1 millimeter

About 1 centimeter

Water boils (100° C)

Normal body temperature (37° C)

Water freezes (0°C)

About 1 Kilogram

5

Observing

How do you observe?

You use your senses when you observe. Your senses are seeing, hearing, touching, smelling and tasting.

You can use your eyes to look at an apple. You can pick it up and feel it with your hands. You can listen to the sounds it makes when you bite into it. You can smell it and taste it when you eat it.

Practice Observing

Materials

 classroom objects

Follow these steps

1. Choose an object. Look at its color, shape, and size. Observe as many things as you can with your eyes.

2. Use your object to make sounds. Listen carefully.

3. Touch your object. Observe how it feels.

4. Draw a picture and write words to tell what you observe about your object.

Thinking About Your Thinking

Draw a picture of something you can observe by smelling or tasting.

Communicating

How can you communicate?

There are many ways to communicate. You communicate when you talk. You also communicate when you draw, write, act something out, or make a chart or graph.

Practice Communicating

Materials

 paper    crayons

Follow these steps

1. Draw a picture of an animal that walks.
2. Draw a picture of an animal that swims.
3. Draw a picture of an animal that flies.
4. Tell how these animals are alike and different.

Thinking About Your Thinking

Are your drawings the same as your classmates?
How did they describe their animals?

Classifying

How can you classify?

Classifying means sorting or grouping things by their properties. You can classify things by physical properties. Shape, color, and texture are some physical properties. You can classify things by whether they are living or nonliving.

Practice Classifying

Materials

 magazine pictures   yarn

Follow these steps

1. Cut out pictures of living things and nonliving things.

2. Make 2 yarn circles.

3. Classify the pictures. Put pictures of living things in one circle.

4. Put pictures of nonliving things in the other circle.

5. Tell about each picture.

Thinking About Your Thinking

How are all the pictures in each group alike?
How are pictures in the two groups different?

Estimating and Measuring

How can you estimate and measure length?

When *you* measure length, *you* find out how long something is. You can estimate before *you* measure. When *you* estimate, *you* tell about how long *you* think something is.

You can use different units to measure length. You can use a centimeter or inch ruler. You can use paper clips, math cubes, or other objects that are all the same size.

Practice Estimating and Measuring

Materials

 paper clips / classroom objects

Follow these steps

1 Work with a partner.

2 Estimate the length of a book. Record on a chart like this one.

3 Measure the length of a book. Record.

4 Estimate and then measure the length of a pencil, school box, or other objects. Record.

Thinking About Your Thinking

Would you use paper clips or a ruler to measure how tall you are? Why?

> Book
> Estimate. _____ paper clips
> Measure. _____ paper clips
>
> Pencil
> Estimate. _____ paper clips
> Measure. _____ paper clips

Inferring

What does it mean to infer?

You infer when you make a conclusion or a guess from what you observe or from what you already know.

You can infer from what you observe with your sense of hearing, seeing, touching, smelling, or tasting.

Practice Inferring

Materials

flashlight

 classroom objects

Follow these steps

1. Work with a partner.

2. Choose an object. Do not let your partner see it.

3. Shine a flashlight on the object. Make a shadow on the wall.

4. Have your partner infer what made the shadow.

5. Take turns.

Thinking About Your Thinking

How were you able to infer what made the shadow? How did what you already know help you infer what the object was?

Predicting

How do you predict?

When you predict, you tell what you think will happen. If you observe something carefully, you may be able to make better predictions.

Practice Predicting

Materials

 3 magnets   paper clips

Follow these steps

1 Use a chart like the one below.

	I predict.	I observe.
1 magnet		
2 magnets		
3 magnets		

2 Push one magnet into a pile of paper clips.

3 Count how many paper clips stick to the magnet. Record.

4 Stick three magnets together. Push them into a pile of paper clips.

5 Count how many paper clips stick to the magnets. Record.

6 Predict how many paper clips will stick to two magnets.

7 Record how many paper clips stick to two magnets.

Thinking About Your Thinking

What would happen if you used more magnets?

Making Definitions

How do you make a definition?

To make an definition, you use what you already know to describe something or tell what something means.

A good definition can help someone understand or guess the object you are describing.

Practice Making Definitions

Materials

 pan balance

Follow these steps

1. Think of what you know about a pan balance. Write a definition of a pan balance.

2. Use the glossary in your science book. Look up **pan balance**. Write the definition.

3. Compare the two definitions. How are the definitions alike? How are they different?

Thinking About Your Thinking

Write a new definition of a pan balance. Use your own words.

Making and Using Models

What can you do with a model?

You can use a model to show what you know about something. A model can also help others learn about the thing that the model represents.

Practice Making and Using Models

Materials

safety goggles   clay   crayons

construction paper   pipe cleaners

Follow these steps

1. Put on your safety goggles.

2. Make a model of an animal.

3. Use the model to show ways the animal can protect itself.

4. You can make a habitat for your animal.

Thinking About Your Thinking

How is your model like a real animal? How is it different? How does the model show how your animal protects itself?

Giving Hypotheses

Why do you ask questions and give hypotheses?

You can ask questions to try to understand something. When you give a hypothesis, you make a statement. Then you can test it to see if it is correct.

Practice Giving Hypotheses

Materials

 masking tape

Follow these steps

1. Can you jump farther from a standing position or with a running start? Tell what you think. This is your hypothesis.

2. Test the hypothesis. Work with a partner. Make a starting line with masking tape.

3. Stand behind the line. Jump as far as you can. Your partner can use masking tape to mark the landing spot.

4. Stand far behind the line. Make a running start and jump when you reach the line. Have your partner mark the landing spot.

5 Make each jump 4 times. Take turns with your partner.

6 Did you jump farther from a standing position or with a running start?

Thinking About Your Thinking

Was your hypothesis correct? Why or why not? If your hypothesis was not correct, change it to make it correct.

Collecting Data

How do you collect and interpret data?

You collect data when you record what you observe. You can use pictures, words, graphs or charts to display data.

You interpret data when you use what you have learned to explain something or answer a question.

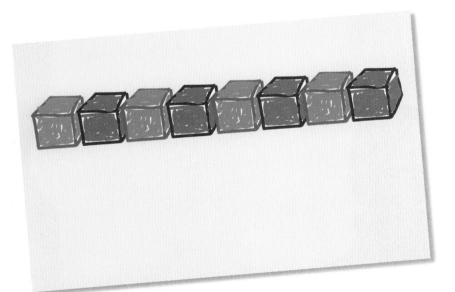

Practice Collecting Data

Materials

Snap Cubes

Follow these steps

1. Work with a partner.

2. Have your partner use Snap Cubes to make a pattern.

3. Tell about your partner's pattern. Predict what colors will come next. Continue the pattern.

4. Draw a picture of the pattern. Display it for others to copy.

5. Collect data. Record how many different patterns your classmates made.

Thinking About Your Thinking

Do the activity again. Make a pattern with numbers instead of colors.

Controlling Variables

What does it mean to control variables?

You identify and control variables when you do an activity and change just one thing. The thing you change is called the variable. A variable can be almost anything. Only one variable changes at a time.

Practice Controlling Variables

Materials

 I block   Snap Cubes

pan balance

Follow these steps

1. Predict how many Snap Cubes it takes to balance a block.

2. Put a block on one side of the pan balance.

3. Put one snap cube on the other side of the pan balance.

4. Add one snap cube at a time until the pan balance is level.

5. Record. How many Snap Cubes does it take to balance one block?

6. Draw a picture to show what happened. Tell about your picture.

Thinking About Your Thinking

What is the variable in this activity?
How did you change the variable?

Experimenting

How do you experiment?

When you do an experiment, you plan an investigation to answer a problem. This is also called testing a hypothesis. After an experiment, you make conclusions based on what you learn.

Practice Experimenting

Materials

 cup of water   yellow food coloring

 blue food coloring   plastic spoon

Follow these steps

Problem

Does yellow food coloring change blue colored water?

Give Your Hypothesis

If you add yellow food coloring to blue colored water, will the color of the water change? Tell what you think.

Control the Variables

Add the same number of drops of food coloring both times.

Test Your Hypothesis

Follow these steps to do the experiment.

1. Add water until your cup is half full.

2. Add 6 drops of blue food coloring to the water. Stir.

3. Predict what will happen when you add yellow food coloring to the water.

4. Add 6 drops of yellow food coloring to the water. Stir. Observe.

Collect Your Data

Make two drawings. Draw the cup with blue water. Draw another picture to show what happened after you added yellow food coloring.

Tell Your Conclusion

Compare your results and hypothesis. What happened when you added yellow food coloring to the blue water?

Thinking About Your Thinking

What do you think would happen if you added 6 more drops of yellow food coloring to the water?

Endangered Plants and Animals

Some plants and animals are endangered. That means that very few of them are living. People all over the world are working to protect many endangered plants and animals.

Endangered Plants

► Prickly Poppy
New Mexico, U.S.A.

▼ Black Lace Cactus
Texas, U.S.A

▲ Thistle
California, U.S.A.

Endangered Animals

▲ Indian Elephant
Indonesia

Tiger
India ▼

Silverback Gorilla
Africa ▼

Terrariums

A terrarium is a container with soil in it. It has plants in it. It can also have animals, such as lizards, toads, salamanders, and snakes. A lid on top keeps enough water inside. A terrarium is a habitat that has everything the plants and animals need.

Aquariums

Aquariums have water in them. Fish can live in an aquarium. People take care of the fish by feeding them and keeping the water clean. Snails and plants can live in an aquarium too. An aquarium is a habitat that has everything they need.

The thermometer shows how warm the water is.

The heater keeps the water warm.

The filter keeps the water clean.

The air pump puts air into the water.

Adaptations

Adaptations are parts or behaviors of a plant or animal that help it stay alive.

The pitcher plant has leaves that trap the insects it uses for food. ▶

◀ The spines of the cactus prevent it from being eaten by animals. The cactus also has a thick stem that holds water for a long time. This helps it live in the desert.

◀ Sharp claws help the armadillo dig burrows and tunnels in the ground. The armadillo also has a special shell that protects its body.

The porcupine has sharp quills that protect it from enemies. ▶

◀ Very good eyesight helps the hawk see things from high in the air. The hawk also has a sharp beak that helps it catch and eat food.

Dinosaur Time Line

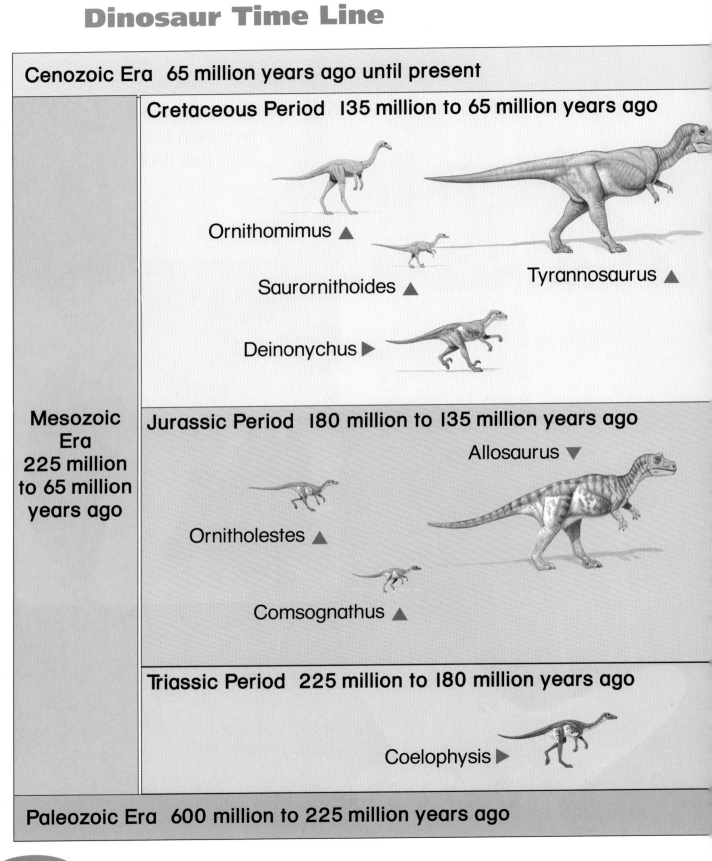

Cenozoic Era   65 million years ago until present

Mesozoic Era 225 million to 65 million years ago

Cretaceous Period   135 million to 65 million years ago

Ornithomimus ▲

Saurornithoides ▲

Tyrannosaurus ▲

Deinonychus ▶

Jurassic Period   180 million to 135 million years ago

Allosaurus ▼

Ornitholestes ▲

Comsognathus ▲

Triassic Period   225 million to 180 million years ago

Coelophysis ▶

Paleozoic Era   600 million to 225 million years ago

Dinosaurs lived on the earth for millions of years. This time line shows some kinds of dinosaurs and when they lived.

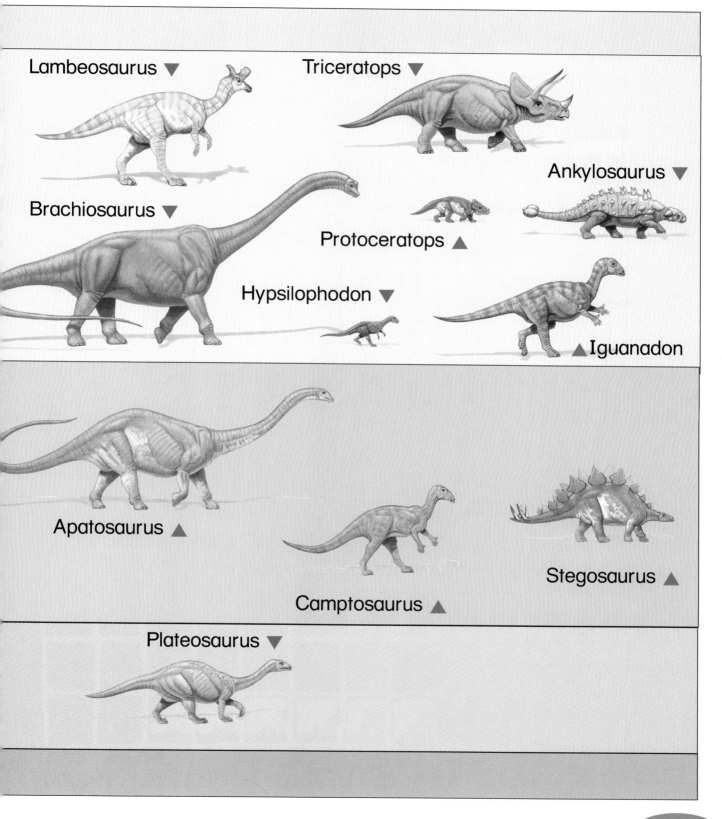

Lambeosaurus ▼

Triceratops ▼

Ankylosaurus ▼

Brachiosaurus ▼

Protoceratops ▲

Hypsilophodon ▼

▲ Iguanadon

Apatosaurus ▲

Stegosaurus ▲

Camptosaurus ▲

Plateosaurus ▼

Using Graphs

The children in room 7 chose which dinosaur they liked best. The graphs show how many children chose each dinosaur.

Picture Graph

In this picture graph, each means one child.

Favorite Dinosaur								
Tyrannosaurus	🧒	🧒						
Lambeosaurus	🧒	🧒	🧒	🧒	🧒	🧒	🧒	🧒
Brachiosaurus	🧒	🧒	🧒	🧒	🧒	🧒		

Bar Graph

In this bar graph, one box is filled for each child.

Favorite Dinosaur								
Tyrannosaurus	▨	▨						
Lambeosaurus	▨	▨	▨	▨	▨	▨	▨	▨
Brachiosaurus	▨	▨	▨	▨	▨	▨		

Circle Graph

This circle graph shows that two children like the Tyrannosaurus best and six children like the Brachiosaurus best. How many children like the Lambeosaurus best?

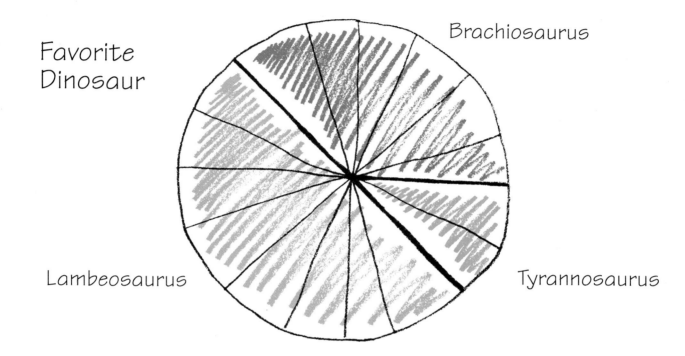

Favorite Dinosaur

Brachiosaurus

Lambeosaurus

Tyrannosaurus

Look at these pictures. Which of these dinosaurs does your class like best? Make a graph to find out.

Allosaurus ▼

Triceratops ▼

Stegosaurus ▲

Map of Plant Products

This map of the United States shows where different plant products grow. Look at the key. It shows what the products are.

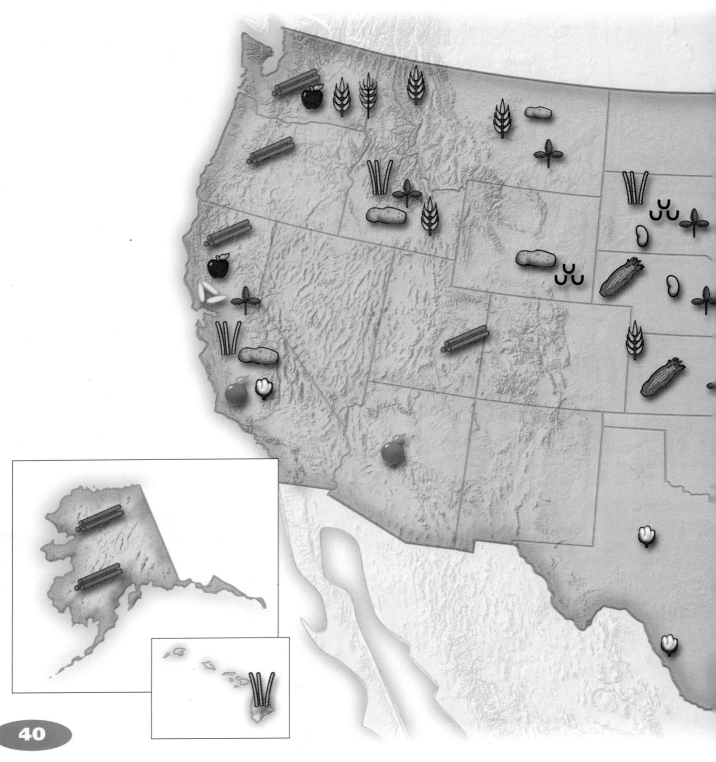

Find your state on the map. What products grow there or nearby?

- alfalfa
- apple
- barley
- corn
- cotton
- oats
- orange
- peanuts
- potato
- rice
- soybean
- sugar
- timber
- wheat

Physical Changes

A physical change is a change in how something looks. It can be a change in the size, shape, or state of matter. A physical change does not change what something is made of.

◀ When you fold paper, you change its shape. This is a physical change.

When you paint an object, you make a physical change. ▼

Chemical Changes

A chemical change takes place when one kind of matter changes to a completely different kind of matter.

When nails rust, a chemical change takes place. ▼

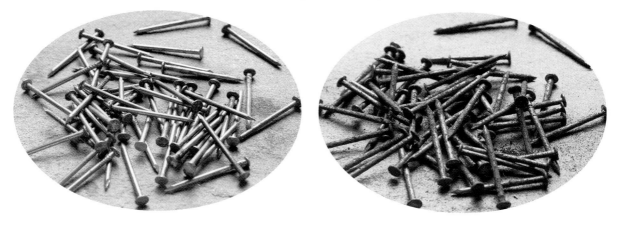

◀ Air causes silver to tarnish. This is a chemical change.

Simple Machines

A tractor and a car are both machines. Did you know that a hammer and a can opener are machines too?

These workers use some kinds of **simple machines** to build a house. Simple machines make work easier.

Wheel and Axle
A wheel and axle is a simple machine made of a wheel attached to an axle, or rod. As the wheel turns, the axle moves.

Inclined Plane
A ramp is an inclined plane. It has a flat surface and one end is higher than the other. An inclined plane makes it easier to move things up or down.

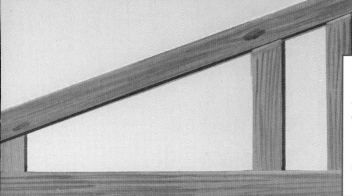

Pulley

A pulley is a simple machine with a wheel and a rope. A pulley can move a heavy object up or down.

Lever

A lever can be used to take a lid off a box. Pushing down on one end of a lever lifts the object on the other end.

45

What is a Globe?

A globe is a sphere with a map on it. The blue
places on the globe show water. The rest is land.
Do you see more water or land on the globe?

Layers of Earth

If you could cut Earth in half, you would see that it is made of layers. The crust is the outside layer. It is the thinnest layer. It is made of rocks and soil. The mantle is the middle layer. It is a hot layer of rocks. The core is the inside of the earth. The outside part of the core is liquid. The inside part is solid. The core is the hottest part of Earth.

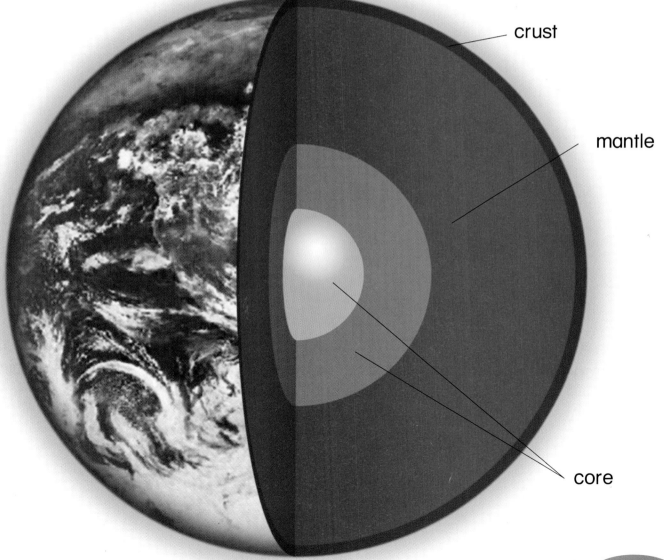

crust

mantle

core

The Ear

You hear sound because sound travels through your ears.

1 Sound enters the outer ear.

2 Sound moves through the tunnel.

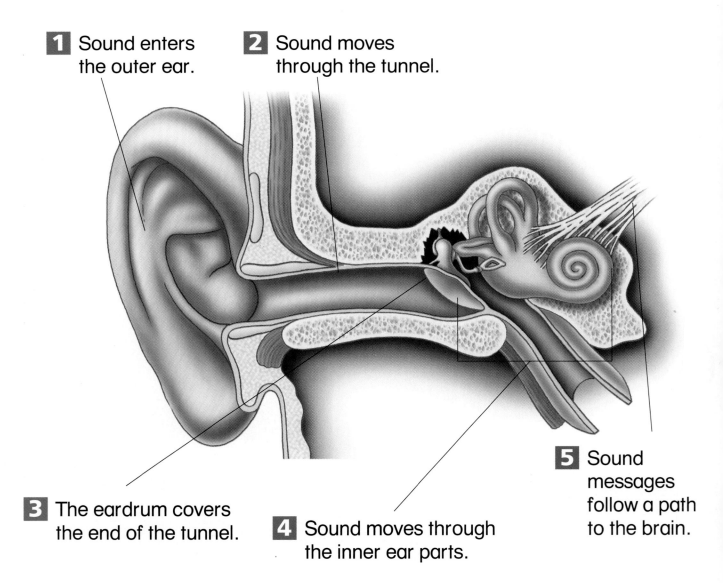

3 The eardrum covers the end of the tunnel.

4 Sound moves through the inner ear parts.

5 Sound messages follow a path to the brain.

Muscles and Bones

Your body has many muscles. Muscles help your body move. Your body also has many bones. Bones hold your body up. Bones move when muscles pull them.

Using Measuring Tools

You can use tools to measure how long something is. Most scientists measure length in centimeters or meters.

Measure length with a metric ruler.

1. Find a pencil. Line up the eraser of the pencil with the end of the ruler.

2. Look at the tip of the pencil. Find the centimeter mark that is closest to the tip of the pencil.

3. About how long is the pencil? Record.

Measure length with a meter stick.

What is the length of your classroom? Measure with a meter stick.

Measure length with a tape measure.

Find something round in your classroom. Use a tape measure to measure around it.

Using a Thermometer

A thermometer measures the temperature. When the temperature gets warmer, the red line moves up. When it gets cooler, the red line moves down.

Some thermometers have a Celsius and Fahrenheit scale. Most scientists use the Celsius scale.

Measure temperature with a thermometer.

1. Put a thermometer in a cup of cold water.

2. Observe the red line in the thermometer.

3. Put the thermometer in a cup of warm water.

4. Observe the red line again.

5. How did the red line in the thermometer change?

Using a Pan Balance

A pan balance is used to measure mass. Mass is how much matter an object has. Make sure the two sides of a pan balance are level before you use it.

Measure mass with a pan balance.

1. Choose two objects. Which one do you think has more mass?

2. Put an object on each side of the pan balance.

3. Which side of the pan balance is lower? The object on the low side has more mass than the object on the high side.

Using a Measuring Cup

You can use a measuring cup to measure volume. Volume is how much space something fills up. Most scientists use containers marked with milliliters to measure volume. The letters mL stand for milliliters.

Measure volume.

1. Find the 100 mL line on the measuring cup.

2. Put the measuring cup on a flat surface.

3. Move your head so that your eyes are even with the 100 mL line.

4. Pour water in the cup until it is even with the line.

Using a Calculator

A calculator can help you do things, such as add and subtract. This chart shows how much paper a school recycled each month. Use a calculator to figure out how much paper they recycled in all.

1. To add a number, press the number. Then press the ➕ sign.

2. Do this for each number in the chart.

3. When you have added all the numbers, press the ＝ sign.

4. The answer should be 98.

Month	Paper Recycled in kilograms
September	7
October	12
November	13
December	9
January	11
February	14
March	9
April	15
May	8

Using a Computer

You can learn about science at a special Internet website. Go to **www.sfscience.com** .

1. Use the mouse to click on your grade.

2. Find a topic you would like to learn about. Click on that topic.

3. You can click on an arrow to go to another page. You can also click on words with lines under them.

4. Tell about 3 things that you learned at the website.

1,000 B.C.	725 B.C.	450 B.C.	175 B.C.	100 A.D.

450 B.C.
People fly the first kites.

250 B.C.
The heavy plow
is invented.

200 B.C.
Archimedes shows how
to use levers and pulleys.

1000 B.C.
People learn to make
tools from iron.

50 B.C.
The wheelbarrow
is invented.

105 A.D.
The first
paper is
made in
China.

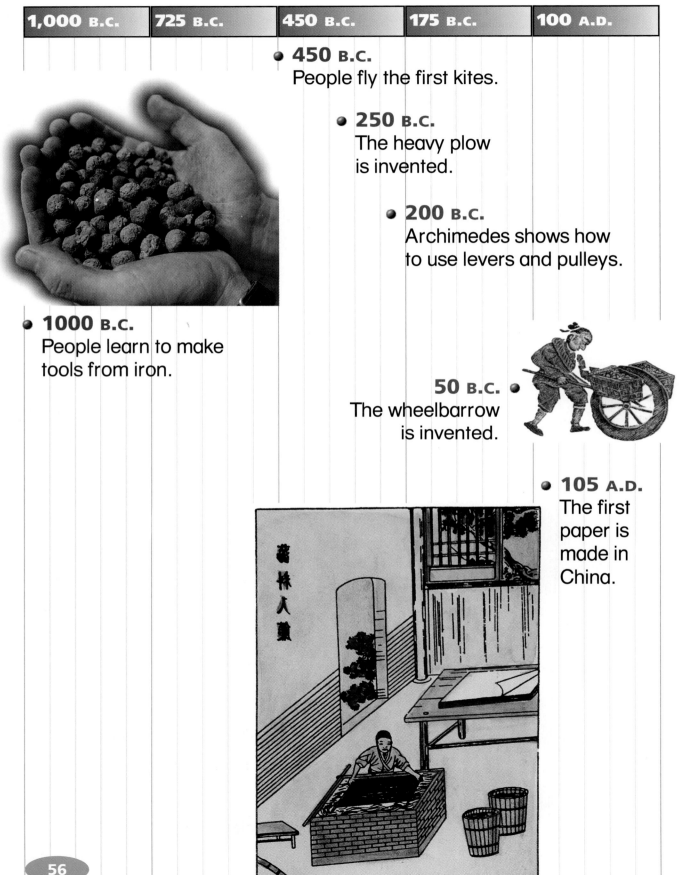

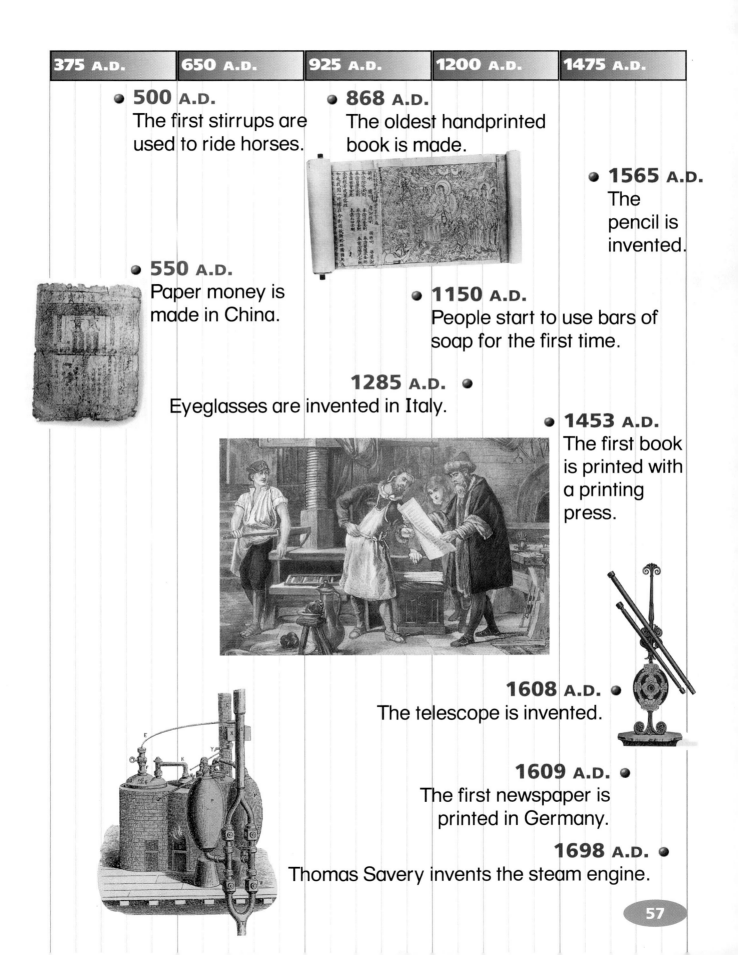

500 A.D.
The first stirrups are used to ride horses.

868 A.D.
The oldest handprinted book is made.

1565 A.D.
The pencil is invented.

550 A.D.
Paper money is made in China.

1150 A.D.
People start to use bars of soap for the first time.

1285 A.D.
Eyeglasses are invented in Italy.

1453 A.D.
The first book is printed with a printing press.

1608 A.D.
The telescope is invented.

1609 A.D.
The first newspaper is printed in Germany.

1698 A.D.
Thomas Savery invents the steam engine.

1752
Benjamin Franklin proves that lightning is electricity and invents the lightning rod to protect buildings from lightning.

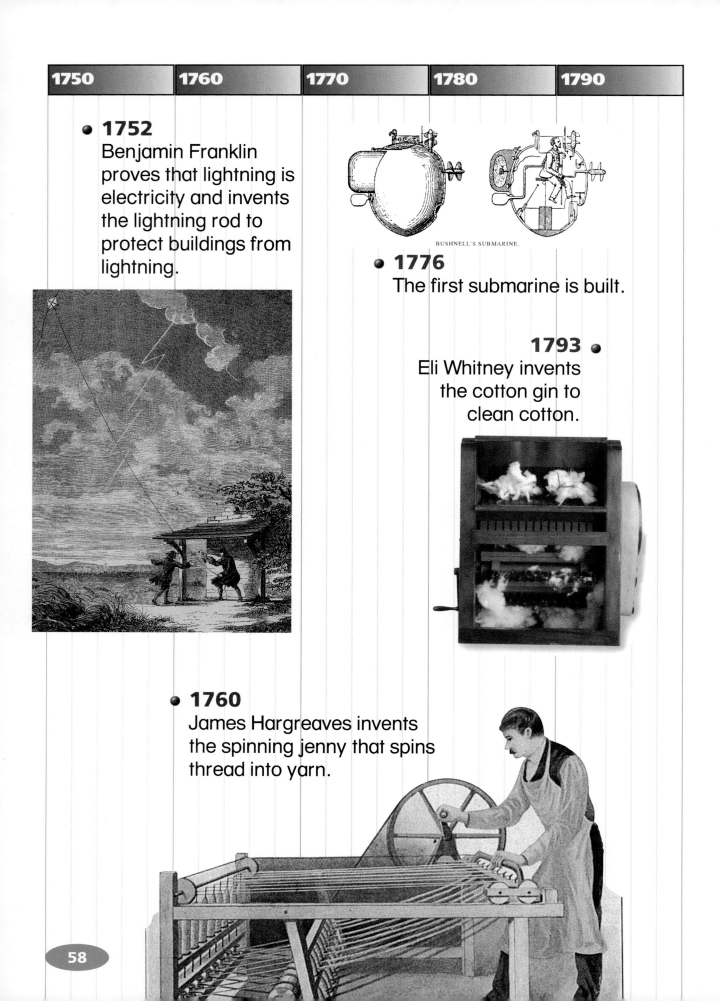

BUSHNELL'S SUBMARINE.

1776
The first submarine is built.

1793
Eli Whitney invents the cotton gin to clean cotton.

1760
James Hargreaves invents the spinning jenny that spins thread into yarn.

1800
Alessandro Volta invents the battery.

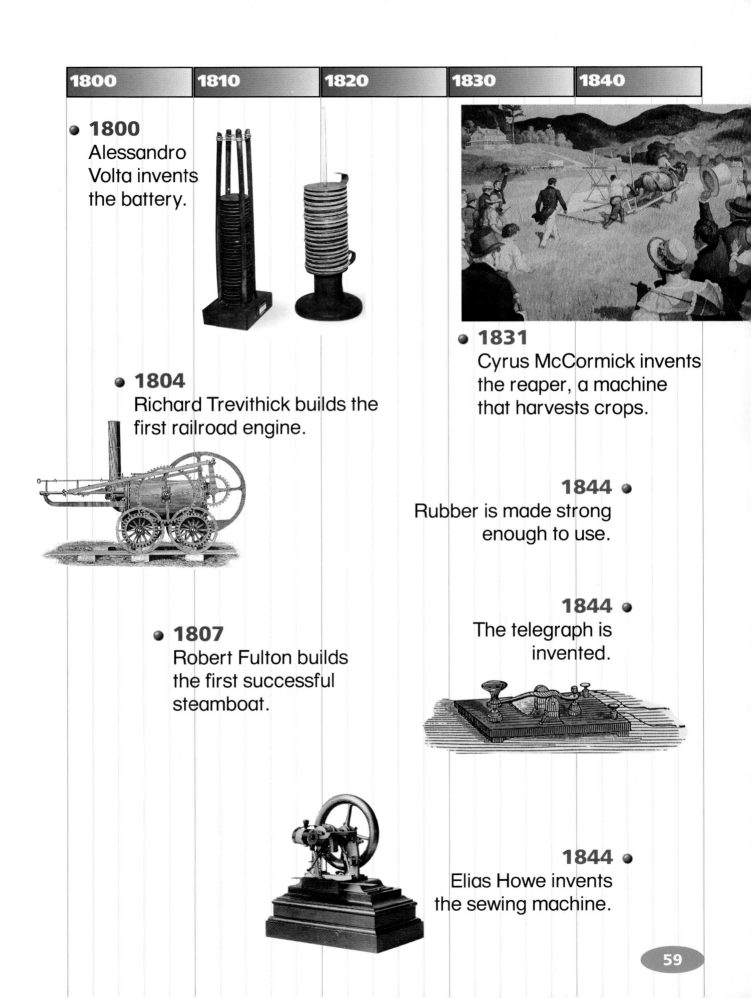

1804
Richard Trevithick builds the first railroad engine.

1807
Robert Fulton builds the first successful steamboat.

1831
Cyrus McCormick invents the reaper, a machine that harvests crops.

1844
Rubber is made strong enough to use.

1844
The telegraph is invented.

1844
Elias Howe invents the sewing machine.

1856
Henry Bessemer shows
how to make strong steel.

1861
Coast to coast communication in
the U.S.A. is made possible with
the telegraph.

1858
The first rubber eraser is put on the end
of a pencil.

1857
The passenger elevator is invented.

1861
Nicolaus August Otto makes the
first engine powered by gasoline.

1863
James Plimpton makes the
first set of roller skates.

1865
The first fax machines
are used.

1873
The typewriter
is invented.

1876
The first telephone call is made.

1884
The fountain pen is invented.

1884
The first roller coaster is built.

1885
The car that uses gasoline is invented.

1877
The record player is invented.

1893
The zipper is invented.

1889
The first dishwasher is invented.

1896
George Washington Carver, a scientist, makes many products from peanuts.

1879
The light bulb is invented.

32
USA

George Washington Carver

61

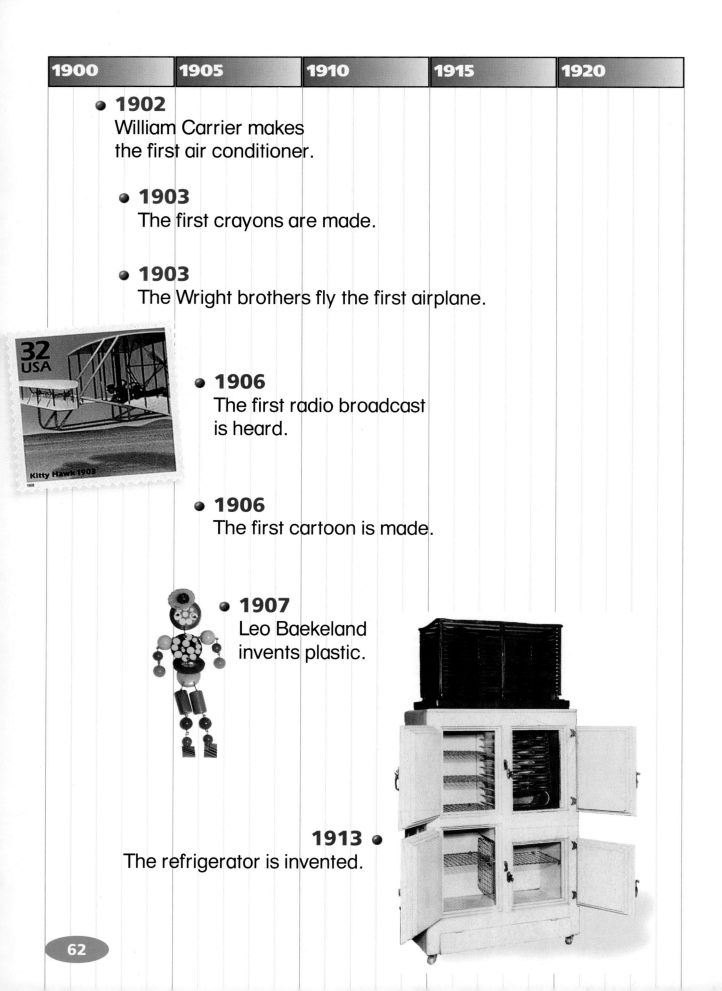

1900 | **1905** | **1910** | **1915** | **1920**

1902
William Carrier makes
the first air conditioner.

1903
The first crayons are made.

1903
The Wright brothers fly the first airplane.

32 USA
Kitty Hawk 1903

1906
The first radio broadcast
is heard.

1906
The first cartoon is made.

1907
Leo Baekeland
invents plastic.

1913
The refrigerator is invented.

1925
Masking tape is invented.

1927
Philo Farnsworth demonstrates the first television.

1928
Sir Alexander Fleming discovers penicillin.

1930
Clarence Birdseye introduces frozen foods.

1931
The Empire State Building is built.

1940
Nylon is invented.

1941
Les Paul builds the first electric guitar.

1946
ENIAC, the first computer, is built.

1947
The microwave oven is invented.

1948
The telephone answering machine is invented.

1954
Color television is invented.

1957
The Soviet Union launches Sputnik, the first satellite into space.

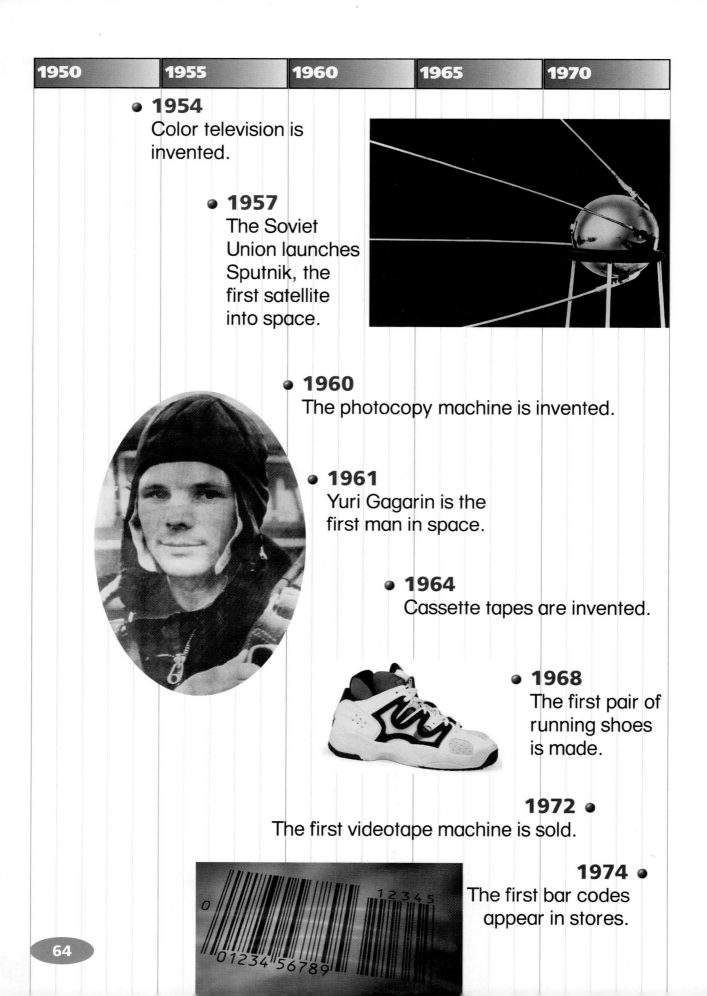

1960
The photocopy machine is invented.

1961
Yuri Gagarin is the first man in space.

1964
Cassette tapes are invented.

1968
The first pair of running shoes is made.

1972
The first videotape machine is sold.

1974
The first bar codes appear in stores.

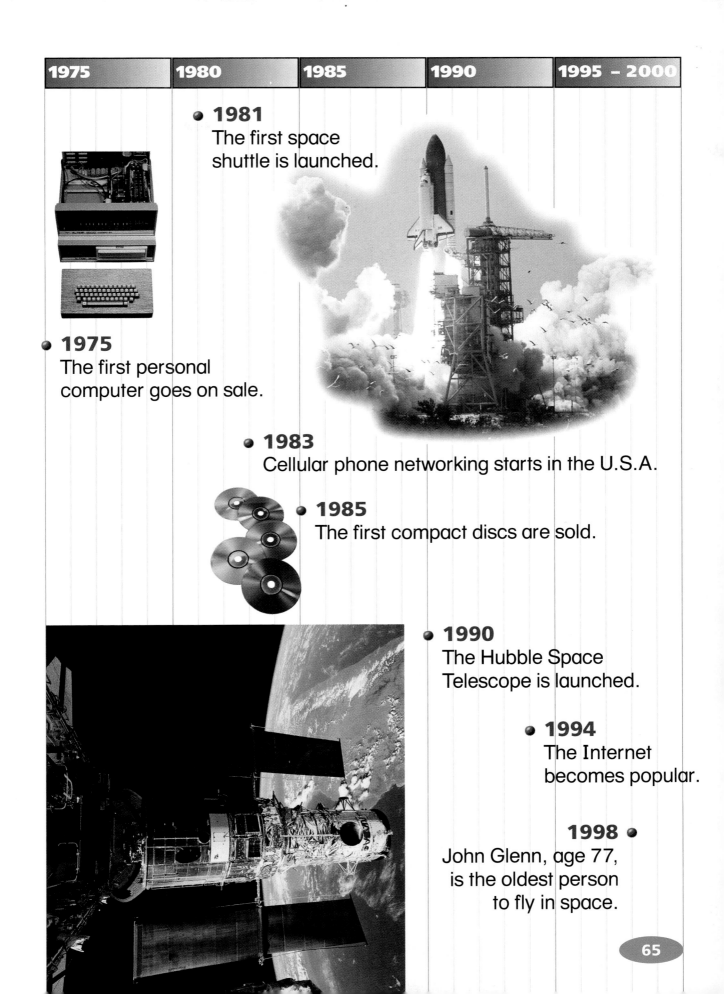

1975 | **1980** | **1985** | **1990** | **1995 – 2000**

1981
The first space
shuttle is launched.

1975
The first personal
computer goes on sale.

1983
Cellular phone networking starts in the U.S.A.

1985
The first compact discs are sold.

1990
The Hubble Space
Telescope is launched.

1994
The Internet
becomes popular.

1998
John Glenn, age 77,
is the oldest person
to fly in space.

Glossary/Index

A

adaptation, 34, 35. An adaptation is a part of or a behavior of a plant or animal that helps it stay alive. The webbed feet on a duck are an adaptation that help it swim.

amphibian, A28. An amphibian is a kind of animal. Amphibians live some of the time in water and some of the time on land. Frogs, toads, newts, and salamanders are amphibians.

anemometer, C28, C44. An anemometer measures how fast the wind is blowing.

animal, A28. An animal is a living thing. Most animals can move around on their own. Animals eat plants or other animals.

aquarium, 33. An aquarium is a tank or glass bowl in which living fish, other water animals, and water plants are kept

artery, D11, D16. An artery is a tube in the body that carries blood away from the heart.

astronaut, C54. An astronaut is a person who travels into space.

attract, B50, B60. Attract means to pull toward.

B

bones, 49. Bones are the hard part of the body. Bones hold the body up. Bones move when muscles pull them.

brain, D6, D16. The brain is a part of the body that is inside the head. The brain controls what the body does. It helps people move, think, feel, and remember.

C

camouflage, A42, A44. Camouflage is a color or shape that makes an animal hard to see.

cause, B44. A cause is a person, thing or event that makes something happen.

chemical change, 43. A chemical change causes matter to become a different kind of matter.

chrysalis, A34, A44. The caterpillar makes a covering called a chrysalis.

circuit, B56, B60. Electricity travels in a path called a circuit.

compost, C20. Compost is a mixture of plant wastes that rot. Compost can be added to soil to help plants grow.

condenses, C38, C44. When water vapor condenses, it changes from a gas to a liquid.

core, 47. The core is the center part of Earth.

crater, C50, C60. A crater is a hole in the ground that is shaped like a bowl. Rocks from space crashed into the moon and caused craters to form.

crust, 47. The crust is the outer layer of Earth.

D

digestion, D26, D30. The process of breaking down food is called digestion.

dinosaur, A52. A dinosaur is an extinct animal that lived millions of years ago. There were many different kinds of dinosaurs.

drought, C43, C44. A drought is a long period of time with no rain.

E

Earth, C48. Earth is the planet we live on. Earth is the third planet from the sun.

earthquake, C15. An earthquake is the shaking of the ground.

effect, B44. An effect is an event that is caused by an earlier event.

electricity, B56. Electricity is a form of energy. Electricity is used for lights, television, toasters and many other things.

endangered, A38, A44, 30, 31. When a plant or animal is endangered, it means that very few are living.

erosion, C12, C24. Erosion happens when soil or rock is carried away by water, wind, or other rocks.

esophagus, D28, D30. The esophagus is the part of the body that squeezes food down to the stomach.

evaporates, C38, C44. When water evaporates it changes into a gas called water vapor.

exercise, D34, D44. When you are active, your body is getting exercise. Walking, jumping rope, and playing tag are all ways to get exercise.

extinct, A58, A60. An animal that is extinct no longer lives on the earth. The dinosaur is an extinct animal.

F

flood, C43. A flood is a large amount of water on land that is usually dry.

flower, A15, A24. The flower is the part of a plant that makes seeds.

food chain, A40, A44. Plants use energy from the sun to make food; animals eat the plants for food; then other animals eat those animals; this is called a food chain.

Food Guide Pyramid, D22, D30. The Food Guide Pyramid shows the food groups. It shows what foods to eat in order to stay healthy.

force, B46, B60. Force is the push or pull that makes something move.

fossil, A50, A60. A fossil is a print or the remains of a plant or animal that lived long ago.

fuel, C18. Fuel is anything that can be burned to make a fire. Coal, wood, and oil are all fuels.

G

gas, B13, B20. A gas is a state of matter that can change shape and size. Air is made of gases.

germs, D40, D44. Germs are tiny living things. Some germs can make you sick.

globe, 46. A globe is a sphere with a map of Earth on it.

gravity, B48, B60. Gravity is the force that pulls things towards the center of the earth.

H

habitat, A38, A44. A place where a plant or animal lives is its habitat.

hatch, A32. To hatch is to come out from an egg.

heart, D10, D16. The heart is the part of the body that pumps blood to other parts of the body.

L

large intestine, D28, D30. The large intestine is a part of the body. Food that is not digested goes into the large intestine. Then it passes out of the body as solid waste.

lava, C14, C24. Lava is melted rock that comes from inside the earth.

leaves, A15, A24. Leaves are part of a plant. Leaves use light, air, and water to make sugars that plants need to grow.

life cycle, A32, A44. Some animals go through many changes as they grow. These changes are called a life cycle.

liquid, B13, B20. A liquid is a state of matter that can change shape. A liquid takes the shape of its container. Water and orange juice are liquids.

lungs, D10, D11. Lungs are the part of the body that take in air.

M

machine, 44. A machine is a tool that makes work easier.

magnet, B50. A magnet is an object that attracts some kinds of metal.

mammal, A28, A44. A mammal is a kind of animal that usually has fur or hair. Cats, horses, bats, and whales are all mammals.

mantle, 47. The mantle is the middle layer of Earth.

matter, B10, B20. Matter is anything that takes up space and has weight.

minerals, C11. Rocks are made of minerals.

moon, C50. The moon is an object in the sky that revolves around Earth.

muscles, 49. Muscles are the part of the body that gives the body shape and helps the body move. Leg muscles help you run.

N

natural resources, C18, C24. Natural resources are useful materials that come from the earth. Water, forests, oil, coal and gas are all natural resources.

nerves, D6, D16. Nerves are pathways in the body that carry messages to and from the brain.

nutrients, D28, D30. Nutrients are materials in food that people need to grow and stay healthy.

O

orbit, C56, C60. To orbit means to move around another object along a path. Earth and the other planets in our solar system orbit around the sun.

oxygen, D10. Oxygen is a gas we need to breathe. There is oxygen in air.

P

paleontologist, A58, A60. A scientist who studies fossils is called a paleontologist.

pan balance, 52. A pan balance is a tool used to measure mass. Mass is the amount of matter in an object.

phases, C51, C60. The shapes of the lighted part of the moon are called phases.

physical change, 42. A change in the size, shape, state, or appearance of matter is a physical change.

planet, C56. A planet is a body of matter that moves around the sun. The planets in our solar system are Mercury, Venus, Earth, Mars, Jupiter, Saturn, Uranus, Neptune, and Pluto.

pitch, B26, B40. Pitch is how high or low a sound is.

plant, A6. A plant is any living thing that can make its own food from light, air, and water.

pole, B50, B60. A pole is the place on a magnet that has the strongest push or pull.

properties, B8, B20. Some properties of objects are color, shape, and size.

pupa, A34, A44. When a caterpillar is changing inside its covering, it is called a pupa.

R

recycle, C20, C24. Recycle means to use something again.

repel, B50, B60. Repel means to push away.

reptiles, A28, A44. A reptile is a kind of animal. Most reptiles have scales. Snakes, lizards, and turtles are reptiles.

roots, A14, A24. Roots are a part of a plant. Roots take in water and hold plants in the soil.

S

saliva, D26. Saliva is the liquid in the mouth. Saliva helps people chew food and starts the process of digestion.

scatter, A20, A24. Scatter means to spread out.

season, C34. A season is one of the four parts of the year. The seasons are spring, summer, fall, and winter.

seed, A16. A seed is the part of a plant from which a new plant grows.

shadow, B38. A shadow is the shape made when an object blocks the light.

simple machine, End Matter 44, 45. A simple machine is a tool with few or no moving parts that makes work easier. A wheel and axle, inclined plane or ramp, lever, and pulley are four kinds of simple machines.

small intestine, D28, D30. The small intestine is a part of the body that helps digest food. Most digestion takes place in the small intestine.

soil, A8. Soil is the top layer of the earth. Plants grow in soil.

solar system, C46. The sun, the planets and their moons, and other objects that move around the sun form the solar system.

solid, B12, B20. A solid is a state of matter that takes up space and has its own shape. A book and a rock are examples of solids.

source, B28. A source is a place from which something comes.

states of matter, B12, B20. Three states of matter are solid, liquid, and gas.

stem, A12, A15, A24. The stem is the part of a plant that carries water to the leaves.

stomach, D 28, D29. The stomach is a part of the body. Food is mixed in the stomach until it becomes liquid.

T

tadpole, A32, A44. A tadpole is a very young frog or toad. Tadpoles have tails and live only in water.

telescope, C58, C60. A telescope makes objects that are far away look closer.

temperature, C28, 51. Temperature is how hot or cold something is.

terrarium, 32. A terrarium is a glass container in which plants or small land animals are kept.

thermometer, C28, C44, 51. A thermometer measures the temperature.

tornado, C42, C44. A tornado is a very strong wind that comes down from the clouds in the shape of a funnel. A tornado can harm objects in its path.

V

vein, D10, D11. A vein is a tube in the body that carries blood to the heart.

vibrate, B24, B40. Vibrate means to move back and forth. Sound happens when objects vibrate.

volcano, C14. A volcano is a mountain that erupts. When it erupts, lava comes out.

volume, B24, B40. Volume is how loud or soft a sound is.

W

water cycle, C38, C44. The way water moves from the clouds to the earth and back to the clouds is called the water cycle.

water vapor, C38. Water vapor is a form of water in the air. When liquid water evaporates, it changes to a gas called water vapor.

Acknowledgments

Cover Carr Clifton/Minden Pictures

i Bob Daemmrich Photography
iv B Rob Simpson/Visuals Unlimited
v E. R. Degginger/Color-Pic, Inc.
viii T E. R. Degginger/Color-Pic, Inc.
x Myrleen Ferguson/PhotoEdit

Unit A
1 Carr Clifton/Minden Pictures
2 T Vincent O'Bryne/Panoramic Images
2 BR Moshe Alamaro/MIT
2 TL Mike Fizer/Check Six
2 BR Louis Psihoyos/Matrix International, Inc.
3 Silicon Graphics
16 B H. Chaumeton/Nature, France
20 BL Dick Thomas/Visuals Unlimited
22 BR John D. Cunningham/Visuals Unlimited
22 C Holt Studios/Nigel Catlin/Photo
   Researchers
23 CR John D. Cunningham/Visuals Unlimited
23 BL PhotoDisc, Inc.
28 T Glenn Oliver/Visuals Unlimited
28 BR E. R. Degginger/Color-Pic, Inc.
28 C Hal Beral/Visuals Unlimited
28 BR Mary M. Thatcher/Photo Researchers
31 TL Rob Simpson/Visuals Unlimited
31 TR Michael Habicht/Animals Animals/Earth
   Scenes
31 B Richard Day/Animals Animals/Earth Scenes
32 L Gregory K. Scott/Photo Researchers
32 C Harry Rogers/Photo Researchers
32 R Harry Rogers/Photo Researchers
33 T Stephen Dalton/Photo Researchers
33 B Harry Rogers/NAS/Photo Researchers
34 LB Gustav Verderber/Visuals Unlimited
34 L E. R. Degginger FPSA/Color-Pic, Inc.
34 R Dr. E. R. Degginger/Color-Pic, Inc.
35 B Dr. E. R. Degginger/Color-Pic, Inc.
35 T Dr. E. R. Degginger/Color-Pic, Inc.
38 David M. Grossman/Photo Researchers
38 Inset Beth Davidow/Visuals Unlimited
39 Renee Lynn/Photo Researchers
39 Inset Dan Guravich/Photo Researchers
42 Bruce Watkins/Animals Animals/Earth Scenes
50 T Sinclair Stammers/SPL/Photo Researchers
50 BR A. J. Copley/Visuals Unlimited
50 BC E. R. Degginger/Color-Pic, Inc.
50 BL E. R. Degginger/Color-Pic, Inc.
52 B A. J. Copley/Visuals Unlimited
53 CL Francois Gohier Pictures
53 CR Denver Museum of Natural History/Photo
   Researchers
58 Francois Gohier Pictures
59 L Courtesy of the Black Hills Institute of
   Geological Research, Inc., Hill City, SD/Black
   Hills Institute
59 R Rich Frishman/Tony Stone Images

Unit B
1 NASA
2 Background Pete Saloutos/Stock Market
2 T Vincent O'Bryne/Panoramic Images
2 CL A. Gin/Picture Perfect
2 BR Light Vision Confections
3 BR Shark Pod
3 BL Charis A. Crumley/EarthWater Stock
   Photography
33 Stock Market
36 TL Frank Siteman/Rainbow
48 Tony Freeman/PhotoEdit

Unit C
1 Ynoto Campanella/Panoramic Images, Chicago
2 T Vincent O'Bryne/Panoramic Images
2 C University of Bristol, England
2 B David Parker/ESA/SPL/Photo Researchers
3 R NASA
8 BL PhotoDisc, Inc.
10 BL Dr. E. R. Degginger/Color-Pic, Inc.
12 Grant Heilman/Grant Heilman Photography
14 Soames Summerhays/Photo Researchers
15 Carl Frank/Photo Researchers
18 Ron Spomer/Visuals Unlimited
19 Zigy Kaluzny/Tony Stone Images
22 Richard Hutchings/Photo Researchers
28 T Christian Grzimek/OKAPIA/Photo
   Researchers
28 B Rich Iwasaki/Tony Stone Images
34 Inset S. Maslowski/Visuals Unlimited
34 E. R. Degginger/Color-Pic, Inc.
35 Inset Maslowski/Photo Researchers
35 John D. Cunningham/Visuals Unlimited
36 Inset Jeff Lepore/Photo Researchers
36 John Gerlach/Visuals Unlimited
37 Inset Ken Highfill/Photo Researchers
37 D. Cavagnaro/Visuals Unlimited
42 L Keith Kent/SPL/Photo Researchers
42 R Merrilee Thomas/TOM STACK &
   ASSOCIATES
43 R Adam Jones/Photo Researchers
50 NASA
51 all Dr. E. R. Degginger/Color-Pic, Inc.
54 PhotoDisc, Inc.
55 J. T. Trauger(JPL), J. T. Clarke(Univ. of Michigan),
   the WFPC2 science team, and/NASA and ESA
58 BL Mel Lindstrom/Lick Observatory/Photo
   Researchers
58 BR NASA
59 NASA

Unit D
1 Bob Schuchman/Phototake
2 T Vincent O'Bryne/Panoramic Images
2 C Dr. Susan Courtney/National Institute of
   Mental Health
2 Inset-B Davies + Starr Inc./Liaison Agency
3 C BBH Exhibits, Inc.
3 B BBH Exhibits, Inc.
20 Myrleen Ferguson/PhotoEdit
34 Myrleen Ferguson/PhotoEdit
38 Jim Cummins/FPG International Corp.
39 L Don Smetzer/Tony Stone Images
39 R Tony Freeman/PhotoEdit

End Matter
4 Bob Kalmbach, University of Michigan Photo
   Services
30 BL Bob & Ann Simpson/Visuals Unlimited
30 BL Marianne Austin-McDermon
30 TR Paul M. Montgomery
31 T Manoj Shah/Tony Stone Images
31 C John Garrett/Tony Stone Images
31 B Patti Murray/Animals Animals/Earth Scenes
34 T Dr. Paul Zahl/Photo Researchers
34 B John Gerlach/Visuals Unlimited
35 T Norbert Wu/Tony Stone Images
35 C Joe McDonald/Visuals Unlimited
35 B Stephen Dalton/Photo Researchers
42 T Digital Vision
42 BL Lawrence Migdale
42 BR Lawrence Migdale
43 TL Charles D. Winters/Photo Researchers

43 TR Charles D. Winters/Photo Researchers
47 NASA
56 T Cliff Hollenbeck/Tony Stone Images
56 B The Granger Collection, New York
56 B The Granger Collection, New York
57 T British Library
57 CR Corbis Media
57 BR Culver Pictures Inc.
57 BL The Granger Collection, New York
58 T Drawing by F. M. Barber in 1885/Bushnell
58 CL Deutsches Museum
58 CR Smithsonian Institution
58 B Culver Pictures Inc.
59 TL Museo Nazionale Della Scienza & Della
   Tecnica Leonardo da Vinci Milan
59 TR Newell Convers Wyeth/International
   Harvester Company
59 CL Stock Montage
59 B Smithsonian Institution of Physical Sciences
59 C Stock Montage
60 T Culver Pictures Inc.
60 C Otis Elevator Company
60 B Hagley Museum and Library
61 TL Corbis Media
61 TR Culver Pictures Inc.
61 TCR Corbis Media
61 CL Public Domain
61 BL General Electric
61 BR Public Domain
62 TL Public Domain
62 TR Public Domain
62 BL Karen M. Koblik
62 BR Corbis Media
63 T Corbis Media
63 C Public Domain
63 B University of Pennsylvania Libraries
64 T UPI/Corbis Media
64 CR UPI/Corbis Media
64 CR Corel
64 B William Whitehurst/Stock Market
65 TR NASA
65 TL Computer Museum, Boston
65 C PhotoDisc, Inc.
65 B NASA